THE FATHERS
OF THE CHURCH

A NEW TRANSLATION

VOLUME 55

THE FATHERS OF THE CHURCH

A NEW TRANSLATION

EDITORIAL BOARD

ROY JOSEPH DEFERRARI
The Catholic University of America
Editorial Director

MSGR. JAMES A. MAGNER
The Catholic University of America

MARTIN R. P. MCGUIRE
The Catholic University of America

ROBERT P. RUSSELL, O.S.A.
Villanova University

HERMIGILD DRESSLER, O.F.M.
The Catholic University of America

BERNARD M. PEEBLES
The Catholic University of America

REV. THOMAS HALTON
The Catholic University of America

WILLIAM R. TONGUE
The Catholic University of America

REV. PETER J. RAHILL
The Catholic University of America

SR. M. JOSEPHINE BRENNAN, I.H.M.
Marywood College

EUGIPPIUS

THE LIFE OF SAINT SEVERIN

Translated by
LUDWIG BIELER
*University College
Dublin, Ireland*

with the collaboration of
LUDMILLA KRESTAN
*Acting Secretary
Österrischische Akademie der Wissenschaften
Vienna, Austria*

THE CATHOLIC UNIVERSITY OF AMERICA PRESS
Washington, D. C. 20017

NIHIL OBSTAT:

REVEREND HARRY A. ECHLE
Censor Librorum

IMPRIMATUR:

✠ PATRICK A. O'BOYLE, D.D.
Archbishop of Washington

June 29, 1965

The *nihil obstat* and *imprimatur* are official declarations that a book or pamphlet is free of doctrinal or moral error. No implication is contained therein that those who have granted the *nihil obstat* and the *imprimatur* agree with the content, opinions, or statements expressed.

Library of Congress Catalog Card No.: 65-12908

Copyright © 1965 by
THE CATHOLIC UNIVERSITY OF AMERICA PRESS, INC.
All rights reserved
ISBN 978-0-8132-2827-3 (pbk.)

CONTENTS

		Page
Preface	. . . .	vii

INTRODUCTION:

    I. Eugippius: Life and Writings 3
   II. Saint Severin 11
  III. Church of Noricum 39

LETTER TO PASCHASIUS 47

MEMORANDUM 57

LETTER TO EUGIPPIUS 101

POEM: ON THE DAY OF SAINT SEVERIN . . . 105

EXCURSUS 111

INDICES 121

v

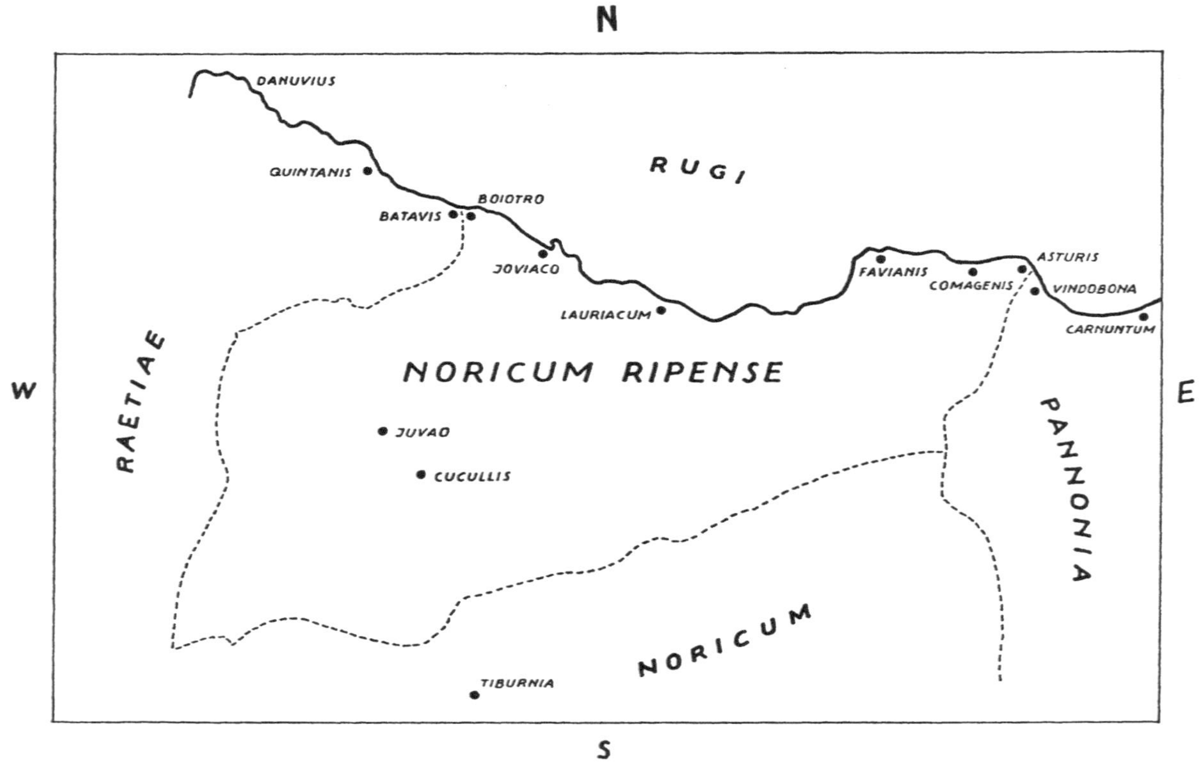
N
W
E
S
DANUVIUS
RUGI
QUINTANIS
BOIOTRO
BATAVIS
JOVIACO
LAURIACUM
FAVIANIS
COMAGENIS
ASTURIS
VINDOBONA
CARNUNTUM
RAETIAE
NORICUM RIPENSE
PANNONIA
JUVAO
CUCULLIS
NORICUM
TIBURNIA

Preface

 UGIPPIUS' BOOK ON ST. SEVERIN holds a place of its own in hagiographical literature. Not only is it a great human and spiritual document, in which the saint's personality shines brightly through all the conventions of the *genre*, it has a quality that is even rarer. Seldom has a hagiographer been so familiar with the scene of his hero's life or so able to recreate this scene before the eyes of his readers; and since of this scene no other record has survived, the importance of the work as an historical source is unrivaled.

This text has been studied most intensively in Austria. For the Austrian, it is what Tacitus' *Agricola* is for the Briton— the earliest literary record of his country's past. There exist about a dozen translations into German by Austrian writers, and numerous learned studies of its several aspects.

However, interest in this text is not restricted to a single country. The case of Noricum, where Severin spent the years of his mature life, must in many respects have been symptomatic, and may, therefore, be used to supplement our picture of the late Roman period in other provinces with regard to which information is not so detailed.[1] When all is said, St. Severin as a man is so great a figure that he deserves to be studied in his own right.

The only English translation that has so far been published is that by George W. Robinson. This excellent piece of work leaves little room for improvement. It is rather in matters of interpretation that the authors of the present volume may claim some advance beyond their predecessor—be it only in present-

---
1 Cf. my comparison of St. Severin and St. Patrick, in *Irish Ecclesiastical Record*, 5. ser., 83 (1955) 161-166. For a parallel between St. Severin and St. Nynias (Ninian), cf. P. Grosjean, *Analecta Bollandiana* 76 (1958) 377.

ing to readers of English the results of recent research in Austria, Germany, and Italy.

Our common interest in Eugippius dates back to those prewar days when Dr. Krestan and I were fellow-students at the University of Vienna. Dr. Krestan afterwards wrote an essay on the social and ecclesiastical conditions of St. Severin's Noricum. This essay, which was never published, together with materials collected more recently, Dr. Krestan has placed at my disposal for the present purpose. Introduction and notes are based largely on Dr. Krestan's work, and not a few passages of the text have been reconsidered in the light of her conclusions. For the ultimate formulation of our views and for the English translation, I alone must take the responsibility. The version of the English translation of the Bible used throughout is the Douay.

Special thanks are due to Dr. Rudolf Noll of Vienna, who generously helped with publications from his unique collection of Severiniana, and who had also the great kindness to read the manuscript and to make a number of valuable suggestions. At the final stage of preparing the manuscript for the press, he has again put us under a very special obligation by communicating, in page proof, his revised edition of Eugippius, which has since been published.

Let this endeavor be a tribute to my native country, and to the saint who came to live there fifteen hundred years ago!

Ludwig Bieler

SELECT BIBLIOGRAPHY

Texts:
Knoell, P. *CSEL* 9.2 (Vienna 1886).
Migne, J. P. *PL* 62.1167-1200 (taken from *Acta Sanctorum Jan. 1.* [Antwerp 1643] 488-497).
Mommsen, T. *MGH Script. Rer. Germ. in usum scholarum* (Berlin 1898). Reprinted with an Appendix and revised by W. Bulst in *Editiones Heidelbergenses* 10 (Heidelberg 1948).
Noll, R. *Eugippius, Leben des hl. Severin. Lateinisch und Deutsch. Anhang: Denkmäler des frühen Christentums in Oesterreich* (Linz 1947). 2. ed. Berlin 1963 (Schriften u. Quellen der Alten Welt 11). [Quoted 'Noll' and 'Noll²' respectively.]
Sauppe, H. *MGH Auct. Antiquiss* 1.2 (Berlin 1877).

Translations:
Robinson, G. W. *The Life of Saint Severinus by Eugippius.* English translation with notes (Cambridge [Mass.] 1914).
Schuster, M. *Eugippius, Leben des heiligen Severin.* German translation with notes (Vienna 1946).

Secondary Works:
Baldermann, H. 'Die vita Severini des Eugippius, 1. Teil,' *Wiener Studien* 74 (1961) 142-155.
Bardenhewer, O. *Geschichte der altkirchlichen Literatur* 5 (Freiburg im Br. 1932) 220-224.
Baudrillart, A. *St. Séverin, apôtre du Norique* (Paris 1908).
Büdinger, M. 'Eugippius, eine Untersuchung,' *Sitzungsberichte der Wiener Akademie der Wissenschaften, phil.-hist. Klasse* 91 (Vienna 1878) 793-814.
Bulst, W. 'Eugippius und die Legende des heiligen Severin. Hagiographie und Historie,' *Die Welt als Geschichte* 1 (Stuttgart 1950) 18-27.
Cappuyns, Dom M. 'Eugippius,' in Aubert-Van Cauwenbergh, *Dict. Hist. Géogr. Eccl.* 15 (Paris 1963) 1376-1378.
Chapman, Dom J. *Notes on the Early History of the Vulgate Gospels* (Oxford 1908).
Diessner, H. T. 'Severinus und Eugippius,' *Wissensch. Zeitschrift der Martin-Luther-Universität Halle-Wittenberg* 7 (1957) 1165-1172 (= *Kirche und Staat im spätrömischen Reich* [Berlin 1964] 155-167).
Dopsch, A. *The Economic and Social Foundations of European Civilization.* English translation by M. G. Beard and N. Marshall (London 1939).
Kramert, K., and E. K. Winter. *St. Severin: Der Heilige zwischen Ost und West* (Klosterneuburg 1958); E. K. Winter, *Studien zum Severinsproblem* (ibid. 1959). [Quoted in my notes as 'KW 1' and 'KW 2' respectively.]
Leclercq, H. 'Eugyppius,' *DACL* 5.1 (Paris 1922) 702-704.
Noll, R. *Frühes Christentum in Oesterreich* (Vienna 1954).
Norden, E. *Alt-Germanien* (Leipzig 1934) 74-78.
Pellegrino, M. 'Il Commemoratorium Vitae Sancti Severini,' *Rivista di Storia della Chiesa in Italia* 12 (1958) 1-26.
Saria, B. 'Forschungsbericht (1940-1950): Noricum und Pannonien,' *Historia* 1 (1950) 438-486.

Sommerlad, T. 'Die Lebensbeschreibung Severins als kulturgeschichtliche Quelle,' *Wirtschaftsgeschichtliche Untersuchungen.* Heft 2 (Leipzig 1903).
Wattenbach-Levison. *Deutschlands Geschichtsquellen im Mittelalter. Vorzeit und Karolinger.* Heft 1 (Weimar 1952) 44-49.
Zeiller, J. *Les origines chrétiennes dans les provinces danubiennes de l'Empire romain* (Paris 1918).
Zeiss, H. 'Die Donaugermanen und ihr Verhältnis zur römischen Kultur nach der *Vita Severini,*' *Ostbayrische Grenzmarken* 17 (1928) 9-13.
Zibermayr, I. *Norikum, Bayern und Oesterreich* (Munich-Berlin 1944) 1-66.

N.B. Reference to the *Commemoratorium* of Eugippius is made by figures only, which indicate chapter and paragraph. Epist. Eugipp. = Epistola Eugippii (prefixed to the main text); Epist. Pasch. = Epistola Paschasii (appended to the text).

EUGIPPIUS
THE LIFE OF SAINT SEVERIN

INTRODUCTION

I. EUGIPPIUS: LIFE AND WRITINGS

UGIPPIUS[1] lives in our memory mainly as the biographer of St. Severin, the 'Apostle of Noricum.' In the ecclesiastical world of his day, however, he seems to have been a figure of some importance. He was abbot of a monastery at Castellum Lucullanum near Naples. There the remains of St. Severin had been deposited, and to him the foundation was dedicated. From Isidore of Seville (d. 636), we learn that Eugippius gave his monks a rule which he left them 'as his (spiritual) bequest.'[2] He had an extensive correspondence with prominent ecclesiastics of the time; we still read letters addressed to him by Fulgentius, bishop of Ruspe, by Dionysius Exiguus (who dedicated to him his Latin version of Gregory of Nyssa's work 'On the State of Man'), and by Fulgentius Ferrandus, deacon of Carthage;[3] his correspondence with the Roman deacon, Paschasius, will be discussed in connection with his Life of St. Severin.[4] The two letters of Ferrandus, written in 533, gave a *terminus a quo* for Eugippius' death.

Among these documents, the letter of Fulgentius of Ruspe[5] is of particular interest. The bishop asks Eugippius to have a

---

1 The name, spelled also Eugipius or Eugepius, seems unique, and defies etymology.
2 *De viris illustribus* c. 26, p. 44 Dz. This Rule has not survived. Mommsen, p. viii, suggests that Isidore may have misinterpreted a passage in the hymn to St. Severin (cf. p. 105), line 22, where Severin, not Eugippius, is said to have given his monks a rule. The hymn, however, seems to be of a later date than Isidore: Wattenbach-Levison, p. 48.
3 For references, cf. Mommsen, p. ix.
4 Below, pp. 6ff.
5 Epistle 5 (PL 65.344ff.).

number of books transcribed for him from the volumes in his monastery. Eugippius had collected a library; in this he was possibly a model for his younger contemporary, Cassiodorus, who had known him personally. There was, however, one important difference between the two collections. Cassiodorus gave a prominent place to the ancient classics; the interests of Eugippius were strictly ecclesiastical. Cassiodorus, not without an undertone of disapproval, calls Eugippius 'a man not too well read in secular literature, but steeped in the reading of Holy Scripture.'[6] Eugippius himself modestly disclaims for his own person all 'liberal studies.'[7] The library of Eugippius, another bequest to his monks, continued after his death to be used for taking copies. We know of three books copied from Eugippius' exemplars before the end of the sixth century: a volume of Origen, a volume of the letters of St. Augustine, and a manuscript of the Gospels, copied from a book that was supposed to have been in the hands of St. Jerome.[8]

Both Cassiodorus and Isidore speak of Eugippius also as a writer. Cassiodorus recommends the study of his *Selections from the Works of St. Augustine*, 'in 338 (recte 348) chapters'; Isidore mentions his *Life of St. Severin*. Both works have survived.

The *Selections (Excerpta) from the Works of St. Augustine*[9] were made at the request of 'my Lord, the abbot Marinus,[10]

---

6 *Institutiones divinarum litterarum*, c. 23.
7 Epist. Eugipp. 2.
8 The Origen copy has survived; of the other two, we know indirectly through second copies. For example, the Gospels corrected after Jerome's book *de bibliotheca Eugipi praespiteri* were recopied (in Northumbria?) during the eighth century; this is the famous *Codex Epternacensis* (Paris, Bibl. nat. Lat. 9389): cf. E. A. Lowe, *Codices Latini Antiquiores* 578. On Eugippius' library, cf. L. Traube, *Vorlesungen und Abhandlungen* 1 (Leipzig 1909) 108f.; Dom J. Chapman, *Notes on the early history of the Vulgate Gospels* (Oxford 1908), *passim*.
9 Edited by P. Knoell, CSEL 9.1 (Vienna 1885).
10 His identity has not yet been established, cf. Bardenhewer, p. 223. Büdinger, p. 803f., thinks Marinus was abbot of some other monastery where Eugippius might have lived for some time, possibly Lérins. With Marinus of Lérins, our Marinus had been tentatively identified already by Mabillon. The Selections would then be of an earlier date

and the other holy brethren,' and dedicated to the 'virgin in Christ,' Proba, a relative of Cassiodorus. The purpose of this compilation was purely utilitarian—to provide an easily accessible book of reference to the teaching of the doctor of the Church, who in Eugippius' time was already considered one of the great authorities in theology. 'This book,' says Cassiodorus, 'is read with great profit, because its author has managed to include between two covers what could hardly be found in a large library.' Eugippius himself justifies his endeavor with the difficulty he had in obtaining all the volumes from which his excerpts were made, and with his desire to spare others the same labor.[11] He exploited nearly forty works of Augustine, not counting his numerous extracts from Augustine's letters and sermons. It is difficult to detect in this bulky compilation any definite plan or pattern, except for one thing, which Eugippius emphasizes in his preface, *viz.*, that the first and the last piece (Augustine's Epistle 167 and Sermon 350) are in praise of charity, which is the beginning and end of all Christian teaching. Eugippius asks his future readers and copyists, who might like to include other extracts according to their special interests, never to move these two pieces from their places of honor. That Eugippius' labor met a real need can be guessed from the great number of medieval copies, the earliest of which dates from the end of the seventh or the beginning of the eighth century. Modern scholarship values these extracts mainly as a tool for checking the manuscript tradition of St. Augustine's writings.

Whereas the major opus of Eugippius is derivative, his *Life* —or, to use his own term, his *Memorandum (Commemoratorium)*[12]*—of St. Severin* is of a very personal character. In

than the Life of St. Severin. Cf. Chapman, p. 41, who also elaborates the connection of Eugippius with Lérins, p. 96ff. Pellegrino (p. 13, n. 21), however, observes that *domino meo* was a common enough form of address of bishops, clerics, and even laymen, and that there is no special reason for identifying our Marinus with the abbot of Lérins.
11 Preface, p. 3, Knoell.
12 The word means 'list, conspectus, synopsis,' cf. Bulst, p. 19; Pellegrino, p. 1, n. 1. Eugippius uses *indicium, indicia,* and *commemoratorium* as synonyms, Epist. Eugipp. 2; 11.

his youth Eugippius had been St. Severin's disciple;[13] he had stood at his deathbed;[14] later, he had accompanied the saint's body on its last journey, from Favianis on the Danube down to Naples; at the time of writing, he was head[15] of the monastic community which had gathered around his master.[16]

The idea of writing about St. Severin, so Eugippius tells us,[17] came to him as he witnessed the success of a *Life,* in letter-form, of the monk, Bassus, who had died—recently, it seems—in the south of Italy. This *Letter,* the work of a layman, was circulated privately, and a number of people took copies. Eugippius and his community thought the miracles of their founder should be made known in a similar way. On hearing this, the biographer of Bassus offered his services and approached Eugippius for information. Eugippius, however, had his misgivings, which were probably aroused by the unknown layman's *Letter* about Bassus. Eugippius feared that the work would be written in such an elaborate style as to be almost unintelligible to ordinary readers; and, to judge from the literary fashion of the times, such fears were not unfounded. Eugippius, therefore, drafted a sketch of Severin's life and miracles, and sent it to Paschasius, one of the seven deacons of the Church of Rome and author of a work on the Holy Ghost, which later won the approval of Pope Gregory the Great.[18] Eugippius asked Paschasius to turn his sketch into a book of such form and style as its subject would demand. This request, it seems, was not meant too seriously. Paschasius in

---

[13] Epist. Pasch. 3.
[14] His presence at the saint's deathbed is formally attested by himself (*nobis vix respondentibus,* 43.9; the variant *nostris,* which would exclude Eugippius, has—*pace* KW 2.21—no authority). Personal acquaintance with Severin is strongly suggested by Epist. Eugipp. 10 and Epist. Pasch. 3.
[15] 37.1.
[16] Beyond this, nothing of Eugippius' earlier life is known for certain.
[17] Epist. Eugipp. 1-2.
[18] *Dialogi* 4.40. Paschasius, as St. Gregory also tells us, sided with Laurentius against Pope Symmachus (for which he had afterwards to suffer greatly in Purgatory). Paschasius died before Symmachus (ob. 514). His work on the Holy Ghost against Macedonius has survived (PL 62.1-40).

his reply politely declined the offer on the grounds that the 'draft' of Eugippius served its purpose excellently, and that nothing could be gained by greater elaboration. Eugippius' *Memorandum* is certainly anything but 'casual'; he uses rhetoric deliberately, though in moderation;[19] he observes the rules of prose rhythm;[20] he is aware of certain demands of composition inherent in a literary genre.[21] Eugippius probably meant to ask Paschasius, a highstanding and influential churchman, to write—as we would say nowadays—a 'Foreword' that would give his work a wider circulation. Paschasius' reply, with its highly complimentary remarks, may then be regarded as a response to Eugippius' polite intimation.[22]

---

19 It is written *brevi stilo*, as Isidore says, *loc. cit.*, cf. above p. 3, n. 2. On the rhetorical elements of Eugippius' style (*Kunstprosa*) cf. Bulst, p. 22f.; on his style in general, C. C. Mierow, *Classical Philology* 21 (1926) 327-332.
20 As one expects, prose rhythm in Eugippius is predominantly accentual, with some survivals of the prosodic type: Bulst, p. 22, with bibliographical references.
21 Cf. Epist. Eugipp. 7. The genre referred to (*ut moris est*) is ancient biography, one of the ancestors of Christian hagiography. It is not the one which Eugippius has in mind for his own composition. Apart from the missing account of his hero's birth, childhood, and youth, of which nothing was known, the *Memorandum* follows the established type of Christian 'aretalogy': episode follows upon episode, leading up to the saint's death. But cf. below, p. 8. Typical of hagiography is also the fact that the account of the saint's death is immediately preceded by a list of devotions and austerities which he practiced; cf., for example, Muirchu's *Life of St. Patrick*, Book II, and L. Bieler's comments in *Proceedings of the Royal Irish Academy* 52 C 5 (Dublin 1950) 219f. Other hagiographical features are the bear as guide, ch. 29 (cf. Robinson p. 81; Noll, p. 179); the removal of unwelcome witnesses before a miracle (16.1-3); the obligation of keeping silence as long as the miracle lasts (16.5; 28.4; cf. Noll, p. 178); and the demand that a miracle should be kept secret in the saint's lifetime (13.2; 16.6, following the Lord's example: Mark 1.44; 5.43; 7.36; Luke 5.14; 8.56).
22 In our manuscripts, it is appended to the text as a postscript. Pellegrino (pp. 1-6) is of the opinion that Eugippius made his request in earnest. We might go so far as to consider as probable that Eugippius wished to give Paschasius an opportunity of suggesting improvements and additions (for example, from the oral accounts of Deogratias, Epist. Eugipp. 6). Apparently Paschasius, for whatever reason, preferred to leave the *Commemoratorium* as it stood. That the latter was conceived as a work of literature would be proved, *inter alia*, by the insertion of the *Capitula*—if genuine, but cf. p. 51, n. 11—after the Epistola Eugippii, which serves as a *Praefatio* (Baldermann, p. 147). It is, of course, possible that, on receiving Paschasius' reply, Eugippius

From a formal point of view, Eugippius' *Memorandum* must be classed as hagiographical legend;[23] it differs, however, from the majority of such works by the author's keen sense of reality in re-creating the social and historical background. Further, the episodes from Severin's life which Eugippius tells are arranged normally—as far as this can be checked—in chronological and topographical sequence, from Severin's arrival in Noricum to his death.[24]

Eugippius tells his story most vividly. 'All readers,' says Paschasius,[25] 'will have the impression that he (Severin) is present and, as it were, lives among them.' With equal freshness, Eugippius depicts Noricum and its people.[26] He had spent some time in Severin's company, and knew the country well; it is a fair guess that he was born there as the son of Roman settlers.

All this combines to make the *Memorandum* of Eugippius a first-hand record of the greatest importance. Doubts concerning its value as an historical source have been expressed by A. Dopsch.[27] These doubts have only a limited validity.[28] A strong anti-Arian and a certain anti-German bias—both understandable in a Roman and a Catholic—may have occasion-

---

slightly revised his work. At that stage, he almost certainly added chapters 45 and 46. Emil Vetter's theory, however (Noll,[2] pp. 33-35), that the unrevised text is preserved in the manuscripts of Class II, the revision in those of Class I has, to my mind, not been proved.

23 So, correctly, Bulst, p. 20f. I cannot believe, however, that this text was intended for monastic *lectiones* in any technical sense.
24 Cf. Noll's synopsis, p. 32f., and below, pp. 35-37. The few exceptions are made on typological grounds, cf. Pellegrino, pp. 7-9; Baldermann, pp. 150-152.
25 Epist. Pasch. 2.
26 One has only to compare any page of Eugippius with the summary and generalizing description by Ennodius, *Vita Antonii Lirinensis* 10-14, in order to see the difference. The strong descriptive element in the *Commemoratorium* is all the more remarkable in view of Eugippius's avowed intention to confine himself to an account of St. Severin's miracles as a matter for edification (Pellegrino, pp. 6; 12; 16).
27 *The economic and social foundations of European civilization.* Condensed from the second German edition (Vienna 1923-24) by Erna Patzelt, and translated by M. G. Beard and Nadine Marshall (London 1939) p. 64f.
28 Cf. Zeiss, p. 9; Pellegrino, pp. 22-26.

ally colored Eugippius' attitude; a case in point is his character portrait of Giso, queen of the Rugi. There is, however, no evidence to show that he ever allowed his feelings to interfere with the facts which he relates. One thing must, of course, be kept in mind: Eugippius writes the life of a saint; the historical and social background, so interesting to us, is for him merely incidental. He was probably unaware of, and certainly not interested in, the broader aspect of Odovacar's policy with regard to Noricum and the Rugi,[29] but this does not detract from the value of the factual information which he gives. Neither need his testimony be discredited because of the long interval between the events and their recording. Eugippius, to be sure, composed his *Memorandum* as late as 509/11[30]— twenty-nine years after Severin's death, twenty-three years after the Romans had abandoned Noricum. Yet the extraordinary man and the exciting events would be vividly remembered even after many years—all the more so as Eugippius was then probably at his most impressionable age.[31]

When Severin died, Eugippius would have been in his twenties. He cannot have joined Severin until many years after the latter had arrived in Noricum. For a large part of his account, he would, therefore, depend on older members of the community,[32] among whom a tradition concerning St. Severin had begun to develop. Of this limitation, Eugippius himself gives his readers fair warning.[33]

The little work of Eugippius won a well-deserved popu-

---

[29] Cf. below, p. 26, n. 79.
[30] His Letter to Paschasius is dated two years after the consulate of Inportunus (Epist. Eugipp. 1) which fell in 509. It was in that year that Eugippius read the Life of Bassus.
[31] Eugippius was still alive in 533 (cf. above, p. 3), more than fifty years after Severin's death. He must at that time have been a young man. There is no evidence to show that either Eugippius or some of Severin's senior monks took notes during his lifetime with a view to later publication (Pellegrino, p. 21); 37.1 can certainly not be quoted in support of this opinion.
[32] Cf. Epist. Eugipp. 2.
[33] In two instances, Eugippius gives the names of his witnesses (11.2; 16.6), both times for miracles which the saint had wished to be kept secret as long as he was alive.

larity. It is quoted for its reference to Odovacar by the so-called Anonymous Valesianus, an Italian chronicler who wrote soon after 526;[34] it was known to Paulus Diaconus in the eighth century, and to the author of the *Gesta Episcoporum Neapolitanorum* about 800, to mention the earliest witnesses only.[35] The number of manuscripts is very great; most of these are of either Italian or Austrian and southern German origin. According to Mommsen, these manuscripts fall in several distinct classes, of which only the first one has preserved the genuine text. However, Paul von Winterfeld[36] and, more recently, Emil Vetter[37] have made a case for following more often Mommsen's Class II or some other manuscript or group of manuscripts; in a number of instances, though not in all, they are right.[38]

---

34 Mommsen, *Chronica Minora* 1.314f. (MGH Auct. Ant. 9. 1892).
35 Mommsen, p. x-xi; M. Manitius, *Geschichte der lateinischen Literatur des Mittelalters* 1 (Leipzig 1911) 262; 269; 710. On the later *Nachleben* of this text, cf. now A. Lhotsky, *Anzeiger der Österreichischen Akademie der Wissenchaften*, phil.-hist. Klasse 1954, pp. 279-282.
36 *Rhein. Museum* 58 (1903) 363-370.
37 Noll,2 pp. 27-35.
38 For the convenience of critical readers, I list here the passages where, in my translation, I have abandoned Mommsen's text. I read Epist. Eug. 4 *molis instar parietem* (Vetter); Chapters 15 *quod signum numquam deinceps aqua penitus excedebat* (II) : Chapters 21 *praedixit mox Norici episcopum ordinandum* (combining I and II) ; 1,4 *antiqua* (so Sauppe) *salutis exempla;* 4,4 *inueniunt* (II) ; 8,3 *spem uitae* (II; cf. 12,6 *spes qua uiueret*) ; 8,4 *sic, sic* (II); 9,3 *subrepere* for *subripere* (Welser); 11,4 *satis factionibus* (all manuscripts, defended by L. Traube); 13,1 *ferri* (om. II) *ac petrae* to be deleted as a gloss (Vetter); 14,3 *sanitate recepta* (*percepta* 'realizing that she was healed' would have biblical parallels but does not fit in the context) ; 17,1 *uel abundare bonis omnibus* to be deleted as a gloss (v. Winterfeld); 17,2 *sit* after *notissimum* to be deleted (om. L and II); 19,4 *regis* (*regi*, with some manuscripts, Mommsen) to be deleted as a gloss (Vetter); 19,5 *quantos . . . reperturus . . . numeros* (TMRS); 21,1 *latius excurrente* (II); 22,2 *destituta* (II); 29,2 *per soporem quendam in effigie* (II); 43,2 *infirmis* (II); 44,7 cf. note on translation; 46,6 add < *sunt curati et diuersis obstricti langoribus* > *receperunt . . . sanitatem* (II).

II. SAINT SEVERIN

1. *Noricum before the time of Saint Severin.*[1]

THE NORIC KINGDOM *(regnum Noricum)* in the Eastern Alps was established toward the end of the second century B.C. by Celts, who, led by the tribe of the Norici, had settled there about 400 B.C. and subjected an earlier Illyrian population. As early as the second century B.C., Celtic Noricum had trade relations with Italy, especially with Aquileia. Economic considerations—Noricum was rich in iron ore—as well as the desire for protection against the northeastern hinterland prompted the Romans to give their relations with the Norici a more permanent form; nominally, Noricum was made an ally; in actual fact, it became a sort of protectorate. Finally, in the time of Augustus, Noricum was incorporated in the Roman Empire (15 B.C.).[2]

The transformation of the allied kingdom into a province must be understood in the light of Augustus' far-reaching plans for securing a strategic frontier in the north. Since Caesar, by his conquest of Gaul, had stopped the German advance towards the west, it remained for his heir to block their passage to the south. As the northern frontier of Rome, Augustus chose the Danube. With this end in view, he inaugurated a policy of military conquest, which was carried out by his stepsons, Tiberius and Drusus. The newly conquered territories

---
1 Cf. Noll, *Christentum*, pp. 4-52.
2 According to Cassius Dio 54.20.4, the Norici were 'subdued' by P. Silvius Nerva in 16 B.C. This is rather doubtful. It is more likely that the Roman troops were called by the Norici for their own protection, and that the Roman occupation was the result of a formal treaty between Noricum and Rome (so F. Miltner, cf. Saria, p. 442). As late as 45 A.D., the legal fiction of a *regnum Noricum* was maintained officially.

were organized as the provinces of Raetia, with Vindelicia (Tyrol, parts of Switzerland, and Bavaria south of the Danube), in 15 B.C., and Pannonia (east of the Alps, between Danube and Save), in 9 A.D.[3] Noricum, situated as it was between these two areas, could not be left to its own devices. Its inclusion in Augustus' scheme was imperative—in the interest of military communications if for no other reason. There was, however, no need of conquest. The change, it seems, was effected by a settlement. Noricum, like Pannonia, became an 'imperial' province, that is to say, a province administrated by the Emperor, and not by the Senate; it was governed by a Roman procurator. Otherwise, there seems to have been no immediate change; even the designation of Noricum as *regnum* continued in popular parlance for quite a long time beside the official term 'province.' In the decades immediately after the end of nominal independence, the state of Noricum was that of an occupied territory rather than of a province; it is not before the days of the emperor, Claudius (41-54 A.D.), that the organization of Noricum as a province was seriously undertaken.[4]

These, in the main, were the frontiers of the Roman province of Noricum: in the north, the Danube; in the east, a line starting from Mons Cetius (Wienerwald) at Vindobona (Vienna), and going along the heights of that mountain range and the eastern edge of the Alps down to the Save; in the south, along the Save, and then westwards along the Karawanken and Carnian Alps into the vicinity of Bressanone

---

3 In this year, Pannonia became a province. The country had been first subjected in 35 B.C. For reasons of administration, Pannonia was divided into Pannonia Superior and Pannonia Inferior in the time of the emperor, Trajan (98-117); both were again subdivided under Diocletian (284-305), but this further division is ignored by Eugippius. Raetia was divided into Raetia Prima and Raetia Secunda under Diocletian. Noricum was bordered by Raetia Secunda in the west (15.1) and Pannonia Superior in the east (Epist. Eugipp. 10). Noricum itself was divided under Diocletian into Noricum Mediterraneum (Styria and Carinthia) and Noricum Ripense (Upper and Lower Austria south of the Danube).

4 See above, p. 11, n. 2.

(Brixen); in the west, from Bressanone to the river Inn, and then following its course from the modern Kufstein to Batavis (Passau) on the Danube.

Contrary to the neighboring provinces, Noricum was not very strongly militarized. There was no need for such measures. Neither was its population hostile to Rome as were the newly subjected Raetians and Vindelicians in the west, nor was the country open to enemy invasions as were the lowlands of Pannonia. Whereas in Pannonia, immediately to the east of Noricum, we find the strong garrisons of Vindobona (Vienna), Ala Nova (Schwechat), and Carnuntum (Deutsch-Altenburg), all three within a distance of some twenty miles, we hear only of some minor forts west of the border. It was toward the end of the first century that Domitian began the construction of the great wall (*limes*) along the Rhine and Danube, which continued on the southern bank of the latter down to the eastern frontier of Noricum; this defense-work included an elaborate system of garrisons, forts, and watchtowers,[5] as well as a flotilla on the Danube.

As everywhere, the Romans built in Noricum a net of military roads,[6] some of which led across the Alpine passes.[7]

The inclusion of Noricum in the Roman defense system secured for the country a long period of peace and prosperity. When the Celts of Noricum came in contact with the Romans, they were already a civilized people; they practiced agriculture, cattle-breeding, mining, and a number of crafts; there had also developed the beginnings of town life. They were thus ready for the absorption of the more advanced civilization of Rome.

The progress of civilization is best seen in the number of cities with Roman municipal status that grew on Norican soil,

---

5 These watchtowers were called *burgi*, a word of Germanic origin. The Burgum where Severin retreats (near Mauternbach? 4.7) was probably such a watchtower, then already abandoned.
6 Zibermayr, p. 15f.
7 29.1. Cf. W. W. Hyde, *Roman Alpine Routes* (Philadelphia 1935) 159-184.

e.g., Celeia (Cilli in Yugoslavia); Virunum (near Klagenfurt), which was the seat of the Roman *procurator*; Teurnia (spelled Tiburnia by Eugippius) on the Drave; Aguntum (near Lienz); Iuvavum (Eugippius' Iuvao, the modern Salzburg); and further to the north, Cetium (Sankt-Pölten),[8] Lauriacum (Lorch near Enns), and Ovilava (Wels). These cities were organized in the usual way. They had an annually elected council of four, assisted by a senate of approximately one hundred members for life. Each of these cities controlled an extensive agrarian hinterland.[9] As happened everywhere throughout the Empire, the municipalities of Noricum rivaled with each other in the erection of sumptuous public buildings—fora, temples, baths, theatres, etc. In the private sphere, too, the standards of living were high; central heating, for example, was fairly common.

Another test of Romanization is the spread of the Roman language. Although the genuine Romans in Noricum were at all times a small minority, knowledge of Latin was common throughout the country.

In religious matters, the Romans adhered to their principle of reconciliation. The native cults were allowed to continue beside the official cult of Rome, first and foremost the cult of the Emperor. Some Celtic divinities were even adopted by the Romans; others lived on under a Roman guise.[10] Besides, the

---

8 This identification is now generally accepted, cf. Saria, p. 467. According to an earlier theory, revived by E. K. Winter (KW 2.181-5), Cetium was Mautern, which most scholars since Kenner identify with Favianis (cf. Excursus). However, a Roman milestone (CIL 3.13534), found near the village of Nitzing, apparently *in situ*, gives the distance from Cetium as 26 Roman miles (ACMP / XXVI, read by Kubitschek: *a Cetio milia passuum XXVI*); this, to go by the modern road system, is exactly correct for Sankt Pölten, but not so for Mautern, which is nearly three Roman miles further away. Besides, the Roman inscriptions relating to Cetium (conveniently listed by A. Holder, *Altkeltischer Sprachschatz*, under 'Cetion') give the impression of a purely civilian town, not of a garrison town, which Mautern was in Roman times.
9 For details, cf. Zibermayr, pp. 11-15.
10 For example, the sun-god, Belenus, became Apollo. Cf. Schuster, p. 13f.; Noll, p. 24ff.

merchants and soldiers[11] imported some oriental cults, for example, those of Mithras and of Jupiter Dolichenus. This is part of the religious 'syncretism,' of the merging of different deities and their cults, which is so characteristic of late antiquity.

In course of time, the Norici felt entirely as Romans, all the more so because to their north, across the Danube, there were people who had as yet absorbed little or nothing of that civilization. Such feelings must have been much strengthened by the invasions of the Marcomanni from across the river in the second half of the second century.

After the victory over the Marcomanni under Marcus Aurelius (d. 180) and the peace concluded by his son, Commodus, the defense of Noricum was further consolidated. An entire legion was stationed at Lauriacum (Lorch on the river Enns);[12] the commander of that legion—a person of senatorial rank—was made governor of the province. However, the former prosperity did not return; neither did the feeling of security.

During the third century, and especially during its second half, Noricum was gradually won for the Christian faith. The beginnings of Christianity in Noricum are unknown. Our earliest records date from the persecution under Diocletian: the martyrdom of St. Florian, a retired officer, at Lauriacum (304),[13] and that of bishop Victorinus of Pettau, a well-known ecclesiastical writer.[14] After Constantine's 'edict of toleration' (313), the Church in Noricum was soon reorganized. At the synod of Serdica (343), Noricum (i.e., Noricum Mediter-

---

11 With the frequent shift of legions, soldiers often found themselves in countries far away from their native provinces. Some place-names of Noricum testify to the one-time presence of southern and eastern legions, e.g., Asturis (from Asturia in Spain), or Comagenis (from the Syrian district of Commagene).
12 'Notitia Dignitatum,' *Occident* 34.39. Lauriacum was a regular garrison town since 205 A.D. Under Caracalla, 211-217, the civil settlement at Lauriacum was given municipal status. Its rank as capital of Noricum Ripense (after the older Ovilava) is confirmed by Eugippius, who terms this town *urbs* (30.4; 31.2). Cf. Zeiller, p. 12; Zibermayr, p. 44.
13 Cf. now especially Zibermayr, pp. 17-31.
14 Cf. Bardenhewer 2 (1914) 657-663.

raneum)[15] was represented by a deputation of bishops who supported the cause of orthodoxy against the Arians.[16] The episcopal sees, as was the practice, were established in the towns. The ecclesiastical province of Noricum was under the jurisdiction of the see of Sirmium.[17]

Secretly, pagan rites continued to be practiced even after the anti-pagan decrees of Constantius (341) and Theodòsius (379-395). In some remote places, pagan sacrifices survived even into the time of St. Severin.[18]

The third and fourth centuries, in spite of some retarding factors, are a time of gradual disintegration of Roman power. Noricum was not so immediately affected as were its neighbors. However, the invasion of Raetia by the Alamanni in 213, which some fifty years later resulted in the loss of the country between Iller, Rhine, and the Lake of Constance, and the settlement of the Goths in Pannonia Superior after the defeat of the Roman armies at Adrianople in 381 could not fail to make the situation of Noricum precarious. Things grew worse when in 433 the Huns established their domination over a large part of northeastern Europe. Their king, Attila, had his residence in central Hungary; his western campaign (447-451) led him right through Noricum. Attila's death in 453 brought anything but relief; on the contrary, the Germanic tribes north and east of Noricum, whose movements had been temporarily checked by Attila's power, broke lose again at once, and within a generation put an end to Roman rule north of the Alps.

It is this last phase of the history of Roman Noricum that forms the background to the life of St. Severin.

---

15 Cf. Zibermayr, p. 37.
16 Athanasius, *Apologia contra Arianos*, 1.37; *Historia Arianorum* 28.
17 Not, as is often asserted, Aquileia. Cf. Zibermayr, pp. 35-41, 57-63. It is only after the evacuation of Noricum Ripense, when Noricum Mediterraneum became a province of Italy, that Aquileia was the head of the Norican sees. This view, however, is not shared by R. Egger, cf. Saria, p. 482.
18 Ch. 11.

2. The historical background of St. Severin's life.

The lifework of St. Severin cannot be understood without a study of the conditions—political, social, religious—which prevailed in the Noricum of his time.

One fact stands out as the root of most of the country's ills —the almost complete breakdown of Roman military organization.[1] According to the *Notitia Dignitatum,* the Roman state and army calendar of ca. 400 A.D.,[2] two legions, each under a *praefectus,* were then stationed in the province, the Second Italian (*Secunda Italica*) at Lauriacum and Lentia, and the First of the Norici (*Prima Noricorum*) with two contingents of *milites liburnarii* (river police), one at Adiuvense (*viz. castrum,* probably on the Ybbs, a tributary of the Danube), the other at Favianis ('Fafianae'); *liburnarii* of the Second Italian were stationed at Ioviaco. There were smaller (auxiliary?) units (*cohortes*)[3] under subordinate officers (*tribuni*) at Asturis ('Austuris'), Boiotro ('Boiodoro'), and Cannabiaca, cavalry at Comagenis and at three other places, mounted archers at Lentia and Lacufelicis (Wallsee?). Naval units are listed at Arlape (Erlauf), Comagenis, and Lauriacum. The latter also had a shield factory.[4] In the neighboring province of Raetia Secunda, we hear of a cohort at Batavis and a cavalry unit (*ala*) at Quintanis.

All that was left in Severin's time—as far as the testimony of Eugippius goes—is a small contingent, under a tribunus, at Favianis,[5] and the garrison (*numerus*) of Batavis.[6] Owing to

---
1 We are speaking here of Noricum Ripense.
2 The following details are checked most conveniently in the geographical index to the edition by O. Seeck (Berlin 1876); most of the references will be found in the section 'Occident,' ch. 34 and 35. Cf. also E. Polaschek, RE 33, 1077ff.
3 Cf. R. Egger, *Anzeiger der Österr. Akademie der Wissenschaften,* phil.-hist. Klasse, 1954, p. 107.
4 *Fabrica scutaria,* Occid. 9. 21.
5 4.2.
6 Ch. 20.

the risks of transport,[7] payment had become less and less regular,[8] and the troops, which were largely mercenary, abandoned their posts when the pay stopped.[9] The garrison of Batavis still held out and tried to collect their pay in Italy, but those who went there were killed on their way by bandits. Their comrades who had stayed, together with recruits from among the civilians, seem to have organized a civic guard, but when Hunumund attacked the city, its defenders numbered not more than forty, and were quickly disposed of.[10] The garrison of Favianis had become so small and so weak that its commander, Mamertinus, felt unequal even to the task of dealing with a band of brigands; it needed the encouragement of Severin and his promise of divine assistance to make him act.[11] A little later, the town is found in the possession of the Rugi, as a sort of royal demesne; king Feva 'gives' it to his brother, Ferderuchus.[12] The remaining Roman soldiers were probably absorbed by the troop which the new masters maintained for the security of their possession.[13]

Not a word is said by Eugippius about the Danube fleet, although, as we shall see, navigation on the Danube was common.

Hand in hand with the disintegration of the army, and following from the same cause, went the decay, for lack of repairs, of the fortifications;[14] the Burgum to which Severin often retires[15] is probably the ruin of a watchtower.

---

7 How much the links with the central power were severed may be guessed from the fact that the Italian priest Primenius, who fled from the murderers of his protégé, Orestes, thought it sufficiently safe to take refuge in Noricum: Epist. Eugipp. 8.
8 It was due every four months: Norden, p. 76, n. 1.
9 20.1.
10 22.4.
11 Mamertinus later became bishop (4.2); in this capacity he would have better chances of helping his city even in temporal matters, as did many other ecclesiastical rulers of the period.
12 42.1.
13 Cf. Zeiss, p. 11. A *miles Avitianus nomine* is mentioned there, 44.2; the steward (*vilicus*) of the same paragraph also seems to be a 'Roman.'
14 20.1.
15 4.7.

The towns, left to their own devices, defended themselves as best they could. Most of them were now protected by walls: Comagenis,[16] Favianis,[17] Lauriacum;[18] in Raetia, Batavis[19] and Quintanis.[20] Behind the walls, civilian life went on without too much disturbance. It is only during the later years of Severin's life that the 'upper towns,' i.e., those on the upper course of the Danube, fall victims to barbarian aggression. Not less than eight Roman towns of Noricum Ripense are mentioned by Eugippius, plus Tiburnia, then the capital of Noricum Mediterraneum, and the Raetian towns, Batavis and Quintanis.[21] About some Norican towns known from earlier

---

[16] 2.1.
[17] 22.4.
[18] 30.2.
[19] 22.1.
[20] 15.1.
[21] The terms employed by Eugippius referring to the several localities of Noricum are not as loose as has often been alleged. He does, to be sure, use the non-technical expressions *locus* 'place' and *mansores, habitatores* 'inhabitants.' But when he employs technical language, he is quite consistent. He uses *oppidum* 'township' of Asturis (1.1), Batavis (19.1; 22.1.2; 27.1), Comagenis (1.3; 2.1; 3.1), Favianis (22.4; 31.1; 42.1; also *civitas* 'city,' 3.1), Ioviaco (24.1.3), Iuvao (13.1), Lauriacum (18.1; 27.2; 28.1; 30.1; once, 30.4, *urbs* 'capital'), Quintanis (27.1; more technically still, *municipium* 15.1), Tiburnia (17.1; also *metropolis*, 21.2). The inhabitants of towns *only* are referred to as *cives* 'citizens': of Asturis (1.2), Favianis (4.1), Tiburnia (17.4; 21.2), Lauriacum (18.1.2; 30.1.4), Batavis (19.1; 22.1). Beside towns, Eugippius mentions *castella* 'forts': Cucullis (11.2; 12.1.5) and Quintanis (15.1; 16.1). These two places had developed a civilian settlement near the military garrison; hence, Eugippius speaks of Quintanis also as *municipium* and *oppidum*, and mentions a certain Marcianus as 'citizen' of Cucullis (11.2). On principle, however, 'towns' and 'forts' are clearly distinguished. For example, in 25.2.3 only, the *castella* of Noricum Mediterraneum are said to have been spared by the marauding Alamanni; on the other hand, we hear only of *oppida* paying tribute to the Rugi (31.1.6); in 11.1 and 17.1, *oppida* and *castella* are mentioned side by side as two distinct types of localities, cf. also 30.1. It is only in relation to a *castellum* that Eugippius speaks of *accolae*, people who have settled beside it, under the protection, as it were, of the stronghold: 11.2; 15.1. This is obvious in the case of Cucullis, where the *castellum* was built on a steep hill (Georgenberg), and the civilian town in the plains at its foot: Noll, p. 164f. The third instance of *accolae* in Eugippius occurs in 4.7 *habitaculum quod Burgum appellatur ab accolis;* the name Burgum seems to indicate that Severin's place of retreat was an abandoned fort. (I do not think, as is assumed in the *Thesaurus Linguae Latinae*, that Eugippius uses *accolae* synonymously with *habitatores*.) The open country had its villages (*vici*, cf. 8.2) and other places of less permanent

sources—Cetium,[22] Lentia, and the former capital, Ovilava—Eugippius is silent. This does not necessarily mean that they were no longer in existence, but merely that there was no tradition connecting them with Severin.

The towns, thrown back on their own resources for defense, were not always successful. Comagenis, for example, had concluded a treaty (*foedus*) with a band of Germans—under compulsion, it seems—which made those Germans actually masters of the town;[23] it was through the intervention of St. Severin that it got rid of this burden.[24] The Norican cities along the lower course of the Danube came more and more under the influence of the Rugians, who had temporarily settled north of the river; these towns eventually became their tribute-paying subjects.

Roads would appear to have still been in fairly good condition. The Roman milestones, indicating distances from the chief city of a district, are mentioned repeatedly.[25] We hear a good deal about traveling and the dispatch of letters, not only between Noricum Ripense and Mediterraneum,[26] but also between Noricum and Italy.[27] It would be saying too much that the roads were always safe. A monk and a layman picking fruit only two miles away from Favianis are taken prisoner by some robbers;[28] the soldiers traveling to Italy for

habitation (cf. *locum . . . ad Vineas*, 4.6). Cf. also F. Miltner, *Anzeiger für die Altertumswissenschaft* 2 (1949) 17; Zibermayr, p. 46. (The phrase *civitates et castella* is biblical: Matt. 9.35.)

22 Cetium seems to have lost its municipal status to the strategically more important Favianis: Zibermayr, p. 14.
23 Yet the Romans kept the keys of the gates: 2.1.
24 Ch. 1 and 2. These Germans were hardly Rugians (Zeiss, p. 11); Norden, p. 75 n. 1, referring to an article by R. Egger, *Wiener Studien* 47 (1929) 146ff., suggests that it might have been a band of Goths.
25 4.4; 10.1; 31.2. Some of them may still be seen in their places: Noll, p. 157.
26 17.4; 25.2; ch. 29.
27 Soldiers go to Italy for their pay: ch. 20; a leper from the Milan district travels to Severin: 26.1; oil is imported: 28.2; correspondence between Severin and Odovacar: 32.1; correspondence of Severin with Barbaria of Naples and her husband: 46.1.
28 *Scamarae*, 10.2, a popular expression, found also in Menander, *Protrepticus*, p. 35; Iordanis, *Getica* 58; cf. Mommsen's *Index to Iordanis* (MGH *Auct. Ant.* 5. 1882) 197; Knoell, p. 80.

the garrison's pay are killed. In winter, the roads across the Alps were also dangerous and difficult to pass.[29] Generally speaking, the open country was at the mercy of brigands of all kinds.[30] It was only in the vicinity of towns that the traditional cultivation of the land—farming,[31] cattle-breeding,[32] bee-keeping,[33] and the growing of fruit[34] and vine[35] —was continued. Work in the fields was shared by men and women.[36] However, the Norici of Severin's time could not live on the produce of their land. Leaving aside occasional disasters, such as rust[37] or pests,[38] too often their crops would fall into the hands of plunderers; besides, a substantial portion of the harvest would go to the Rugi by way of tribute.[39] Nori-

---
29 Cf. ch. 29.
30 Ch. 4; 10.
31 Ch. 12; 18.1; 22.4. The arable land was divided into lots, which apparently were private property: 12.4.
32 4.1; 30.4. On the cattle of Noricum, cf. Cassiodorus, *Variae* 3.50 (MGH *Auct. Ant.* 12, p. 104f.); they were 'of rather small size, but better for work than the bigger and higher priced cattle of the Alamanni.' Cattle was kept outside the city walls, except in an emergency (cf. 30.1-4). There is no reference to dairy farming. The normal cooking fat was (imported) oil: 28.2. However, Eugippius mentions details of this kind only in passing, and nothing should be concluded from his silence.
33 This must be concluded from several references to tapers (11.2,3,5; 13.2), cf. Sommerlad, p. 56. It is nowhere intimated that tapers were imported; and to judge from 11.2, their use was fairly common, not only in church, but also at home.
34 10.1.
35 Cf. 4.6, where a locality near Favianis is called *Ad Vineas*. The growing of vine in the provinces developed since the time of the emperor Probus (276-282), who lifted the ban which, until then, had protected the Italian export. With the development of the provinces, the demand for this article had obviously so much increased that it could be met no longer by Italy alone.
36 Cf. 14.3, where female labor in agriculture is said to be 'according to the custom of the province.' Tacitus, *Germania* 25, which has often been quoted in this connection, does not apply. Tacitus says that the land is tilled by the tenants, whereas women and children look after the house. Besides, Tacitus speaks of the Germans, Eugippius of the Celto-Romans of the province of Noricum.
37 18.1.
38 Locusts, ch. 12.
39 17.2. It seems that all payment in fifth-century Noricum was made in kind. Eugippius, to say the least, never mentions money. The tithes which Severin levied for his charities consisted in grain and clothes. Even the payment of the soldiers might have been 'rations' rather than cash: Sommerlad, p. 52.

cum was, therefore, dependent on the import of grain from Raetia, which was shipped on the Inn and Danube; so much dependent, in fact, that even the temporary delay of a cargo by the freezing of the river Inn would cause famine.[40]

The Roman and Romanized population of Noricum tended to live behind the walls of their towns. Only once do we hear of 'Romans' on the countryside—the inhabitants of a village near Favianis, who are kidnapped by the men of Giso, queen of the Rugi, and pressed into slave labor.[41]

Brigandage, however, was not the only danger that arose from the weakening of Roman power, and by no means the gravest. For centuries, the German tribes north and east of the Roman frontiers had been checked by a net of fortifications and by the Roman legions behind them. Now that the country lay open, these tribes were not slow to see their chance. In the neighboring Pannonia, the Goths had already been settled officially on Roman territory. There was nothing to bar their way into Noricum. If they did not invade the western province, except, perhaps, for some isolated groups,[42] one of their reasons was probably the power of the Rugi north of the Danube,[43] who more or less controlled also the territory between the Danube and the Alps.[44]

Freed from vassalage to Attila, the Rugi had entered into an alliance with Rome. As early as 458, we find them fighting for Majorian. There was much friction between the Rugi and their cousins, the Goths. In 468, the leaders (*principes*) of the Goths felt strong enough to deny the Rugian king, Flaccitheus, passage through Noricum Mediterraneum to Italy.[45] In the following year, Flaccitheus, together with other German tribes, engaged in a war against the Goths, but he and his allies were

---
40 Ch. 3.
41 8.2; cf. Zeiss, p. 11.
42 Cf. above, p. 20, n. 24.
43 The residence of their kings would seem to have been near the northern bank of the river, not far from the modern Krems, opposite Favianis.
44 Cf. 8.2; 31.1,4; 42.1. In the west, their sphere of influence did not extend as far as Lauriacum: ch. 30; 31.
45 5.1.

defeated near the river Bolia. The power of the Rugi was temporarily weakened;[46] but a few years later, the Goths left Pannonia and went partly westwards, partly (and with their main force) southwards, where they settled again in the province of Moesia. En route, they besieged Tiburnia in 473.[47]

One of the tribes that had fought against the Goths were the Sciri. After their defeat, a number of them went to Italy as mercenaries; among these was young Odovacar. Passing through Noricum Ripense, he visited Severin and asked for his blessing. Severin is said to have foretold him his rise to power,[48] and later to have prophesied his downfall.[49] Odovacar became king of Italy in 476. He showed great deference to the holy man who had foretold him his future greatness, and after the saint's death gave the Romans of Noricum asylum in Italy.

Equally devoted to Severin was Flaccitheus after he found himself freed from his dangerous neighbors as the saint had prophesied. The same attitude was shown by Flaccitheus' son, Feletheus or Feva, who succeeded his father ca. 475. It seems due largely to the good relations of Severin with the Rugian dynasty that Noricum enjoyed a certain measure of stability and order. Hard masters that they were, the Rugians felt as protectors of the *Romani*—a name which by that time had come to mean much the same as our 'Latins'—against their own less civilized cousins, the Alamanni, the Heruli, and the Thoringi.[50] These tribes were still pagans, whereas the Rugians (perhaps through missionaries from the Goths) had accepted Christianity—be it only in the form of Arianism.[51]

---

46 At that time, Rugians were even occasionally kidnapped by Goths: 5.3.
47 Cf. ch. 17.
48 7.1.
49 32.2.
50 On the Alamanni, cf. above, p. 16. Their raids were dreaded; the biggest one, in 473, brought them as far as Noricum Mediterraneum (25.3). The Heruli are mentioned only once, as destructors of Ioviaco, ca. 477 (24.3). The Thoringi are found near the Danube in the fifth century (cf. 27.3), but were unable to hold that area.
51 Cf. 4.12. Arius (d. 336) denied the *homousia* (equality of divine nature) of the Son with the Father. His doctrine was condemned by the Council of Nicaea, 325.

Being heretics, however, their religion, so far from establishing a bond between themselves and their 'Roman' subjects, would rather tend to make relations strained. It needed all the tact of Severin, whom their king held in great esteem, to find a common platform.[52] This was made all the more difficult by the fanaticism of Feva's queen, Giso, a staunch Arian, who even attempted to rebaptize some of her Catholic subjects.[53] Her portrait as painted by Eugippius is that of a hard and haughty woman, and this she might well have been.[54]

On the whole, however, relations between the two peoples seem to have been fair. The foreigners (*barbari*)[55] were anything but uncivilized, although their civilization was obviously less developed than that of the Roman province. The royal family almost certainly spoke Latin; we never hear of an interpreter.[56] Their material interests are manifested by the presence at their residence of foreign goldsmiths, who, in strict and hard custody, work for the crown-treasure.[57]

Most interesting for the social historian are some references to commerce between Romans and Rugians. The Rugians held weekly markets on their side of the Danube, which were frequented by the Romans of Noricum as a matter of course.[58] In winter, when the Danube was frozen, the ice was crossed by

---

52 Cf. 5.2.
53 8.1. Although only the extreme wing of the Arians developed a baptismal rite of their own (F. Cabriol, DACL 1.2815), the whole sect, it would appear, considered the Catholic baptism invalid.
54 Her type, however, is also a stock character of hagiographical legend. Eugippius' censures (8.4; 40.1; 44.4) seem to spring mainly from his aversion to the fanatical heretic.
55 This word need not have a derogatory connotation; the Germans even applied it to themselves. For Romans, to be sure, the word had an undertone of 'less civilized'; they knew Germans mostly in subordinate positions, as tenants of land, as servants, or as mercenaries (Dopsch, p. 90).
56 Contrary, Gibuld, king of the Alamanni, negotiates with Severin's representative through an intermediary (*internuntius*, 19.4), who receives Severin's letter and hands over the king's reply (Zeiss, p. 11). This *internuntius* is apparently the king's secretary; one thinks of some Arian presbyter.
57 8.3.
58 6.4; 9.1,3. On commerce between Germans and Romans in general, cf. Norden, p. 74, n. 1.

cartloads of goods;[59] at other times, cross-river traffic was by boats.[60] Even in those days, the Danube was the main artery of the country for the conveyance of both goods and passengers.[61] The attraction for Roman merchants of the Rugian markets is proved by the request of the citizens of Batavis that Severin should obtain for them a trading license from king Feva.[62]

Most of the other German tribes are represented as less civilized. Odovacar, visiting Severin, is clad in hides, the traditional costume of the ancient Germans. How precious clothing was to the 'barbarians' may be guessed from the fact that the Goths, when giving up the siege of Tiburnia, by the terms of the treaty (another treaty under pressure!) demanded that they be given a stock of worn clothes which had been collected for Severin's charities.[63] On the other hand, the besiegers of Lauriacum are familiar with the Roman tactics of storming walls by ladders.[64]

The Rugians, then, were an exception to the rule. In Raetia, for example, relations between Romans and Germans left something to be desired.[65] Even the presence of Severin at Batavis and Quintanis, where the population in their distress had called him,[66] had only a temporary success, in spite of the impression he made on king Gibuld.[67] Severin's representatives, the deacon, Amantius, and the priest, Lucillus, were allowed to take home a number of Roman prisoners,[68] but the raids on Roman towns continued. Tired out by these incursions, the people of Quintanis eventually retreated to Batavis;[69]

---

59 4.10.
60 We do not hear, though, of a regular ferry service.
61 3.3; 22.4.
62 22.2.
63 28.2. In the same direction points the testimony of Iordanis, *Getica* 56. In the case of Ferderuchus, 44.1, it is sheer greed.
64 30.4.
65 Zeiss, p. 10.
66 15.2; 19.1.
67 19.2.
68 19.3-5.
69 27.1.

even there, the attack was renewed,[70] and although the Alamanni were defeated, Severin urged the people to retreat further to Lauriacum. Some of the Batavians, who refused to abandon their native soil, were killed soon afterwards during a raid by the Thoringi. We see here, within Severin's lifetime, one brief phase of the 'decline and fall' of the Empire take place before our eyes. At the time of Severin's visit to Cucullis,[71] the 'upper towns' of Noricum Ripense are still standing, but most of the forts are exposed to attacks of the *barbari*; it was a time when the garrisons were still regularly paid, and the *limes* was kept in repair.[72] When Severin stayed at Batavis, things had already begun to change;[73] now (ca. 477), as Zibermayr[74] concludes, the country west of the Enns had to be given up, and Severin could do no better than fall in line with the policy of the day.[75] The retreat to Lauriacum proved wise; the enemy gave up the siege of the town before it had properly begun.[76] When Feva with his army appeared, the Alamanni were already gone. It was possibly his coming that caused them to leave. Through the good services of Severin, a peaceful settlement of the Roman refugees among the Rugians in the lower towns of Noricum was then worked out.[77]

The process of disintegration did not, of course, stop there. At the time of Severin's death (482), only a few towns on the Danube remained.[78] Six years later, Odovacar, having put an end to Rugian power,[79] ordered the Romans of Noricum to

---

[70] 27.2, 3.
[71] Ch. 11; 12.
[72] Cf. 20.1.
[73] *Ibid.*
[74] P. 42.
[75] 28.1.
[76] Ch. 30.
[77] This plausible interpretation of ch. 31 is given by Zibermayr, p. 43f.
[78] 42.1.
[79] Eugippius gives as Odovacar's reason for this expedition the murder of Ferderuchus, brother of King Feva, by Feva's son, Fredericus (43.3,4). This is in itself improbable, and is flatly contradicted by the chronology of the events. The murder of Ferderuchus occurred within a month of Severin's death (482); the first of the two campaigns against the Rugi fell in the year 487 (*Chronica Minora* 1.312f.; 315; Cassiodorus, *Chronica Minora* 2.159). These dates alone exclude the idea of a puni-

leave for Italy, where they would be resettled. A new line of defense had to be taken, which ran along the heights of the Alps.[80] Odovacar's decree was announced by his brother, Hunwulf (Onoulfus), who conducted the (second) Rugian campaign;[81] the evacuation was organized by count Pierius.[82] If Eugippius were to be taken literally, all provincials (*omnes incolae*) left Noricum on that occasion. However, Eugippius himself tells us that the order was given only to the 'Romans.' Most scholars believe that only the Romans and those whose livelihood depended on Roman rule were evacuated—the landowners, the merchants, and the few remaining officials; the small people, for example, the tenants (*coloni*), would stay behind and put up with their new masters. A certain continuity of habitation is proved by archaeological finds, and by the persistence of such place-names as Quintanis-Künzing, Batavis-Passau, Lentia-Linz, Lauriacum-Lorch, Cucullis-Kuchl.[83]

---

tive expedition. Odovacar's Italian kingship had never been recognized by Byzantium; he was accepted only as regent (*patricius*). When Odovacar began to prepare a Balkan campaign, the Byzantine emperor, Zeno (474-491), in order to divert him, incited Feletheus (Feva) to invade Italy. He was prevented by Odovacar's attack. During a battle on the Danube, Feva and his queen fell into captivity; they were sent to Italy, and later put to death. Fredericus escaped and returned to his country. He was defeated, but again escaped and fled to the headquarters of the Ostrogoth king, Theoderic, at Novae in Moesia (cf. 44.4). His plea was certainly one, though not the only, cause of Theoderic's conquest of Italy, which cost Odovacar his throne and his life (489-493; cf. Mommsen, p. vif.; Noll, p. 187f.). The destruction of the Rugian kingdom created a void which was promptly filled by the expanding power of the Heruli; it was perhaps this inevitable consequence of Odovacar's action that made the evacuation of Noricum necessary (Noll, p. 176).

80 Zibermayr, p. 56.
81 44.4.
82 44.5.
83 Cf. A. Nagl, RE 18.527; A. Hauck, *Kirchengeschichte Deutschlands* 1, 3rd-4th ed., (Leipzig 1904) 364; Dopsch, p. 81ff.; Zeiss, p. 13; Saria, p. 486. H. Thaller, *Die Städte der Vita S. Severini im Donauraum*, in: *Beiträge zur älteren europäischen Kulturgeschichte*, vol. 2 (*Festschrift für Rudolf Egger*, [Klagenfurt 1953] 315-321), points out that this continuity of habitation, which is evident in Raetia and in Noricum west of the Enns, does not apply equally to the lower (eastern) part of Noricum Ripense; there the towns seem to have been completely abandoned, but not so the countryside.

3. *The man and his work.*[1]

Even in our endeavor to re-create the scene, a great deal had to be said about the central figure—Severin. Who was that strange man? Nobody ever knew. He had come from the east where he had lived in one of those deserts that were the cradle of monasticism.[2] In obedience to a divine call,[3] he had given up his life of contemplation, and traveled all the way, under great dangers, to the border of Pannonia and Noricum, where a people in distress was looking for spiritual and temporal guidance. He refused to tell even a venerable priest what was his home.[4] His speech betrayed him as a 'true Latin,'[5] but this need not mean anything more than that he was not an easterner, that Latin was his native language. People suspected that he came from a noble family and, in his humility, wished to conceal his parentage.

The date of his arrival in Noricum must fall between the death of Attila (453) and the beginning of the reign of Flaccitheus (ca. 468); a date nearer the latter term seems more probable. The state of Noricum at that moment has already been sketched; but St. Severin's mission cannot be understood fully unless we try to see also the reactions of the people. Their attitude may be described briefly as one of despondency and, at the same time, of obstinacy. There is some evidence also of those petty vices that always crop up in times of want, for example, the hoarding of food,[6] and a general unwillingness to give of the little that was left. Religious life, as we shall see, was richly developed, but most people would be satisfied to

---

1 Cf. Noll, *Christentum*, pp. 53-68; L. Bieler, *St. Severin and St. Patrick: a parallel*, in: *Irish Ecctes. Record*, 5th ser., vol. 83 (1955), 161-166.
2 Epist. Eugipp. 9. On eastern monasticism, cf. H. Leclercq, DACL 2.3140-3165; 11.1791-1831.
3 Epist. Eugipp. 10. E. K. Winter (KW 1.180-183; 2.65; 186; etc.) thinks Severin acted, at least unofficially, along the lines of the Danubian policy of Byzantium. That Severin had a certain Byzantine background is in itself not improbable, but Winter's speculations concerning it belong entirely to historical fiction.
4 Epist. Eugipp. 8-9.
5 *Ibid.* 9.
6 3.2.

observe its externals. We do not hear a word, however, about excesses of either debauchery or intemperance, which were then so common in other parts of the Empire.[7]

Severin saw his first and fundamental task in a spiritual revival; this meant bringing people to a fuller realization of their religion. Everywhere Severin exhorts his congregation to the performance of the good works of prayer, fast, and almsgiving. These he recommends in every emergency, be it illness, or danger to the crops, or an attack of the enemy. Moreover, he urged the people to put all their trust in God, and not in their own precautions, which, as they must have realized, were grossly inadequate. Strengthened by their confidence in divine assistance, the Romans often succeeded unexpectedly—at Favianis,[8] at Batavis,[9] at Lauriacum.[10]

Needless to say, Severin would fight the remnants of paganism where they still persisted, as in Cucullis.[11] His was a militant nature. It cannot be without intention that Eugippius applies to him the time-honored metaphor, 'soldier of Christ,'[12] with such great emphasis. First of all, Severin subdues his own body by prolonged prayers and mortifications.[13] This, according to an accepted manner of speech, is the 'warfare' of the monk.[14] A harder struggle, and a greater victory, it is to conquer one's pride; and we do read about Severin's great humility, of which he gave some striking examples.[15]

But Severin is also a fighter for the Catholic Romans against the Arian or pagan Germans. Fasts, prayers, and works of

---

7 Once we read of robbing a church and desecrating its holy vessels (44.1-3); but this is done by orders of the Arian king, Ferderuchus. The steward, whom he sends first, refuses to obey; the soldier, Avitianus, goes under compulsion, but with a bad conscience, and afterwards quits the king's service and does penance as a hermit.
8 4.4.
9 Ch. 27.
10 Ch. 30.
11 11.2-5.
12 For example, 6.5; 16.2; 18.2; 42.1. As regards the idea, cf. A. Harnack, *Militia Christi* (Tübingen, 1905).
13 1.2; 4.7,9,10; 17.1; 39; 40.1.
14 Cf. 43.5; 35.2 (Bonosus) *quadraginta fere annis in monasterii excubiis perseverans*.
15 4.11, 12; cf. 1.2; 5.1; 6.2; 14.2; Severin declines to be made bishop, 9.4.

charity are the heavenly arms with which alone the enemy can be defeated.[16] This is the power which Severin sets against the inefficient military power (*militia*) of the Empire. The story of Mamertinus' expedition against the brigands[17] is conceived throughout in terms of this contrast; and the repentant Avitianus, formerly a soldier of Ferderuchus, afterwards a hermit, 'changed his service and took up heavenly arms.'[18]

Among the 'arms' of good works, the one on which Severin insisted most strongly was charity. The years of his mature life were a time of distress—a time of want, of danger, of insecurity. In whatever form these evils were present, Severin would challenge them. He is a *Nothelfer*. He averts famine;[19] he sets limits to the flooding of a river;[20] he warns of attacks;[21] he heals the sick, Germans as well as Romans.[22] Of all afflicted people, however, those nearest to his heart are the poor and the captives. He, who fasted rigorously and defied the Norican winter, felt the hunger and nakedness of the poor as if it were his own.[23] It is for their relief that Severin levied tithes. The institution was known from the Old Testament;[24] it was accepted as binding on Christians, at least in theory, but the law was not generally enforced until some time in the sixth century.[25] Severin took the bold step to insist on its fulfillment. He would write even to Noricum Mediterraneum for their tithes in order to bring relief to the more exposed Danubian region.[26] Contrary to the later custom, these tithes were used for no other than charitable purposes. The tithes were paid in kind; they consisted mainly, it seems, in grain and cloth-

---
16 1.4; 2.2; 27.2; 28.1.
17 Ch. 4.
18 *Armis caelestibus mancipatus militiae commutavit officium*, 44.2.
19 Ch. 3; 12; 18.
20 Ch. 15.
21 Ch. 1; 24; 25; 30.
22 A number of illnesses are either described or named: gout (6.1), leprosy (ch. 26), elephantiasis (ch. 33; it is the 'Greek' elephantiasis, a form of leprosy: Schuster, p. 185), eye trouble (ch. 35), a deadly pustule (ch. 38), deafness (45.1), blindness (46.4), severe headache (46.5). Severin himself probably died of pleurisy (43.1; cf. Schuster, p. 189).
23 17.2,3.
24 Cf. Lev. 27.30ff.
25 Sommerlad, p. 48.
26 17.4.

ing.[27] Although Severin knew that for many these contributions were a great sacrifice,[28] he was firm in demanding it. On two occasions, Severin interprets a misfortune as a divine punishment for being slow to give;[29] on the other hand, an heroic effort to deliver the collected alms is rewarded by a miracle.[30]

Equally great was Severin's care for Christian captives. A substantial part of his tithes must have been spent for ransom.[31] Occasionally, he was able to obtain the release of captives by agreement, as from Gibuld, king of the Alamanni.[32] Some of the persons whom he had ransomed seem to have been employed in his service, for example, Maurus whom he made custodian of his basilica of Favianis,[33] or the layman whom he sent across the Danube for relics.[34] One is inclined to assume that these people, together with his monks, were employed also for the administration of his charities.

Even beyond such practical measures, Severin shows himself an apostle of mercy. He frees the brigands captured by Mamertinus, not without a wholesome admonition;[35] he makes even the hard-hearted Giso, who counteracts the merciful intentions of her husband, comply with his requests;[36] he pleads with Feva for a considerate treatment of the Roman refugees.[37]

Severin was not content with appealing to the Christian people at large; he also strove to win adepts for a more perfect life. He seems to have been the first to introduce monasticism to Noricum.[38] His first and most important monastery[39] was

---

27 17.4; 18.1; 29.1; 44.1.
28 Cf. 17.2.
29 17.4; 18.2.
30 Ch. 29.
31 9.1; ch. 10.
32 Ch. 19.
33 Ch. 10.
34 9.1-3.
35 4.4.
36 Ch. 8; cf. also ch. 40.
37 31.5.
38 The monasteries of Noricum mentioned by Eugippius were all founded by Severin. There were monasteries in Raetia, cf. 41.1. Lucillus, at one time a monk under Valentine, the later bishop of Raetia, seems to have afterwards placed himself under the jurisdiction of Severin: 19.5; 44.5; 45.2.
39 4.6; 22.4.

at Favianis;[40] it had a basilica, with a monk in charge (*aedituus*).[41] Another monastery he founded at Boiotro near Batavis;[42] it grew from humble beginnings[43] to a place of some importance.[44] A third one was near Iuvao.[45] Severin used to have a cell of his own (*cellula, oratorium*), separated from the quarters of the other monks,[46] where he could retire for prayer or reading;[47] he joined the community for morning and night prayers (i.e., most probably, Matins and Vespers). His monks were recruited mainly from the Celto-Romans; Bonosus, 'of barbarian stock,' is represented as an exception.[48] A person wishing to become a monk would take a vow.[49] Severin shaped his monks by his own example[50] and by the example and teaching of the Fathers of the Desert.[51] He did not compose a written Rule as was assumed by the author of the hymn in his honor.[52] Severin was a guide of souls.[53] In one particular case, we are informed of this in so many words: Antonius (the later St. Anthony of Lérins) came to him as a young boy. Severin 'petted him with kisses, and in doing so acknowledged

---

40 Perhaps on the site of the present Johanneskirche at Hundsheim: Noll, p. 158. Cf. also p. 37, n. 96.
41 9.3; 10.1.
42 19.1; 22.1.
43 'A retreat (*cellula*) for a few monks,' 19.1. *Cellula* seems to be used as a synonym of *monasterium;* 39.1, even Severin's large monastery at Favianis is called *cellula*.
44 Ch. 36. Cf. C. Rodenberg, *Leben des heiligen Severin von Eugippius* (Die Geschichtsschreiber der deutschen Vorzeit, vol. 4, 3rd ed., Leipzig 1912), 67.
45 14.1. It is characteristic that Severin always founded his monasteries in the vicinity of cities. In this he possibly followed the example of St. Basil. Cf. F. W. Rettberg, *Kirchengeschichte Deutschlands* 1 (Göttingen 1846) 231; Robinson, p. 37, n. 1; Fathers of the Church, vol. 19, p. xi.
46 10.2; 20.2; 39.1.
47 10.2; 20.2.
48 35.1. Cf. Zeiss, p. 12.
49 *Venerabile* or *sanctum propositum,* 1.1; 4.7; 43.6; 44.2. Cf. Schuster, p. 189.
50 4.6 *factis magis quam verbis.*
51 For example, he compares to the wife of Lot, a monk who looks back regretfully on his life in the world: 9.4. The same comparison is found in Athanasius, *Life of St. Anthony,* ch. 20.
52 See below, p. 105.
53 *Spiritalis doctor,* 39.1.

in the boy his future excellences as if they had shown already in the past. For he was not the sort of person to whom anything would be hidden. He announced everywhere with his holy tongue that Anthony would once share his way of life— with the intention, I think, of strengthening the first steps of a tiro by the hopes which he professed to entertain.'[54] He could also be strict when necessary as with the three proud monks at Boiotro;[55] Eugippius even felt that Severin's discipline was in need of some justification.

Eugippius' portrait of St. Severin is, of course, conceived in the manner of hagiographical legend. We readily believe that Severin followed a divine call, not only when he decided to go to Noricum, but also in some of his minor decisions, e.g., in accepting the invitation to Favianis[56] or in returning to this city from his hermitage at the Vineyards.[57] More conventional are the numerous stories about Severin's knowledge of events happening far away;[58] he knows even the miracle of the bear in the Alps![59] The healing miracles are told with deliberate reminiscences of similar miracles worked by the Lord;[60] for the miraculous increase of oil, Eugippius himself refers to the Old Testament model, 2 Kings 4.2-7.[61] As regards Severin's numerous prophecies, especially those of political or military events, it would be idle to speculate as to what may be due to private information, or to natural intuition, or to supernatural revelation; the hagiographer, quite legitimately, refers it all to its ultimate cause. Similarly, one would think, must be understood those passages in which Eugippius describes the power of Severin's personality. When Severin is admitted to the strictly guarded town of Comagenis without questioning,[62]

---

[54] Ennodius, *Vita s. Antonii Lirinensis* 9.
[55] Ch. 36.
[56] 3.1.
[57] 4.6,7.
[58] e.g., 10.2; 17.4; 20.2; ch. 37.
[59] 29.4.
[60] Cf. Noll, pp. 160f., 166f.; on the typology of the raising of Silvinus, cf. L. Bieler, *Archiv für Religionswissenschaft* 32 (1934) 228-245.
[61] 28.3.
[62] 1.4.

there is nothing miraculous implied in Eugippius' words; neither is there in his statement[63] that the robbers, being unable to bear Severin's 'venerable presence,' released their prisoners; more drastic, but equally natural, is the effect of Severin's personality on king Gibuld.[64] It is only in the testimony of those who feel his influence that we occasionally perceive a note of the miraculous. The forts of Noricum Ripense rival with each other to invite Severin because they believe that as long as he is with them they will suffer no harm;[65] here, the presence of the holy man is treasured in much the same way as would be a miraculous relic or other blessed object. In chapter 36.4, Eugippius speaks of the awe (*reverentiae terror*) in which Severin is held after the healing of the three monks who had been possessed by the devil.[66]

Occasionally, Severin met with opposition. That in the beginning, when he was unknown, his advice was not heeded is not surprising. But even later, he often found it difficult to persuade people to take his warnings seriously; even the 'saintly priest,' Maximianus of Ioviaco,[67] was not convinced by his repeated warnings. Events, of course, always proved Severin right.[68]

It is the news about the destruction of Asturis[69] that makes the people of Comagenis believe in Severin's prophetic gift and thus establish his fame in Noricum. Soon afterwards, he is invited to Favianis,[70] and then, one by one, to other places: Cucullis,[71] Quintanis,[72] Batavis.[73]

Opposition to Severin was found particularly among the

---

63 10.2.
64 19.2.
65 11.1.
66 On the miracles of St. Severin in general, cf. Pellegrino, p. 24; Winter, KW 2.190-200.
67 24.2-3.
68 1.5; 24.3; 27.3.
69 1.5.
70 3.1.
71 11.2.
72 15.2.
73 19.1.

local clergy, who did not always take kindly to the stranger. No wonder—what should they think of a man who, without even being a priest,[74] dared to speak to them with divine authority? On one occasion, a priest of Batavis makes himself the spokesman of popular resentment against the fasts and vigils introduced by Severin.[75] His punishment is not delayed for long; during Hunumund's raid of the city, the priest is murdered in the very same place where he has reviled Severin.[76]

This is Severin as seen by the hagiographer. The historian will try to reconstruct from this account the role played by the saint on the political scene. Unconcerned about politics as is Eugippius, he has made our task easy. Reading the sequence of episodes that make up Severin's life, one gets the impression that, for the greater part, these pieces are not strung loosely together as is so often the case in hagiography or are arranged on a purely formal pattern, but that they follow upon one another with a certain logic—the logic of facts which determines every step of Severin's movements. Coming from the east, Severin enters Noricum at Asturis, the frontier town against Pannonia.[77] Failing to persuade the inhabitants that they are in danger, he proceeds to Comagenis, the nearest town to the west, where his advice is followed.[78] He is now invited to Favianis, the chief town of the lower district of the province. There he stays for some time. For doing so, he had good reasons. Not only was Favianis an important place, it lay opposite the residence of the Rugian kings, with whom he so

---

74 On this point, I think, the silence of Eugippius is conclusive. The words (23.1), 'when Severin was reading the Gospel in the monastery of Favianis,' need not imply that he was saying Mass.
75 22.3.
76 22.5. The murder of a priest by pagan Germans (here and 24.3, where Maximianus is hanged by the Heruli) may have had the purpose of destroying a person in whom they thought was invested the magic power of their enemies. According to Ennodius, *Vita s. Antonii* 13, the Heruli, Saxons, and other barbarians, 'who appease their gods with human sacrifice, immolate Christian priests as their choicest victims.'
77 1.1-3.
78 1.4-2.2.

successfully established friendly relations.[79] It is there that Severin founded his first and largest monastery which was to become his headquarters. From there, he is invited to Cucullis and Iuvao.[80] It is the only inland journey of which we know;[81] on the whole, Severin moves along the Danube, in the danger zone. At some later date, Severin is called to Raetia, where things had taken a bad turn: to Quintanis,[82] to Batavis and Boiotro;[83] there he is visited by Paulinus[84] and (most probably) by the leper from Milan;[85] from there he sends his warnings to Ioviaco[86] and his letters to Noricum Mediterraneum.[87] Severin soon realized that, in spite of his influence with Gibuld,[88] he could do very little, and urged evacuation: from Quintanis to Batavis[89] and from Batavis to Lauriacum.[90] There he works the oil miracle and receives the convoy led by Maximus.[91] After the lifting of the siege[92] and the agreement with Feva,[93]

---

79 Ch. 5-7; cf. Noll, p. 37.
80 Ch. 10-14.
81 However, both Cucullis and Iuvao are still situated in Noricum Ripense. Winter's fantastic theory (KW 1.30ff.) that Cucullis, Iuvao, and Quintanis (ch. 15-16) have been substituted for places on the Danube east of Batavis, and that this was done in the interest of the churches of Salzburg and Passau, need not be taken seriously. It is worth noting, however, that the six miracles related in ch. 11-16 are the only ones in the entire work which have no specific historical background.
82 Ch. 15-16. There, it seems, he also prophesied about Tiburnia, 17.4, and received a deputation of the repentant people of Lauriacum, ch. 18.
83 Ch. 19-27. Severin's stay is interrupted by a journey to Favianis (22.4-23.2), in order to escape the raid of Hunumund and to receive the relics of St. John the Baptist, which had been sought for Boiotro but were destined for Favianis. The saint's departure is expressly stated, but not so his return. On this assumption, the difficulties raised by Pellegrino, p. 10, find a simple explanation. Hunumund did not destroy Batavis, and, as it was harvest time, he found in the city and killed only the forty men on guard duty.
84 Ch. 21.
85 Ch. 26.
86 Ch. 24.
87 Ch. 25.
88 19.2-5.
89 Ch. 27.
90 Ch. 28.
91 Ch. 28-29.
92 Ch. 30.
93 Ch. 31.

Severin retires to Favianis, where he seems to have stayed until the end of his life, except for occasional visits to places in the lower district, e.g., the one to Comagenis mentioned by Eugippius.[94] It is at Favianis that Severin died on January 8, 482,[95] and was temporarily buried.[96] Soon after his death, the monastery was plundered by Ferderuchus.[97]

Six years later, when Noricum was evacuated of its Roman population, the saint's body, in fulfillment of his last wish, was lifted and taken to Italy.[98] Although the body had not been embalmed, it was found intact.[99] It was deposited, first, at Mount Feleter (Monte Feltre near San Marino in Umbria); later (after 492), a noble lady by the name of Barbaria, a spiritual friend of Severin, offered a permanent burial place at Lucullanum, near Naples.[100] By authority of Pope Gelasius, the remains of St. Severin were deposited there under the direction of bishop Victor of Naples; the whole town, so we are told, attended the solemn act. In obedience to their master, the community of his monks had kept together. They now settled at his tomb.[101] The 'monastery of St. Severin' is mentioned several times in the letters of Pope Gregory the Great.[102] It was a place of pilgrimage as is attested by the author of the *Vita sancti Willibaldi*.[103] In 902, the relics of St. Severin were transferred to the city of Naples, for fear of a Saracen invasion.[104] A last 'translation' took place in 1807, when the relics

---

94 Ch. 33. The story of the proud monks of Boiotro, ch. 36, is inserted merely by way of illustration. Boiotro had long been abandoned.
95 43.9.
96 On the supposed tomb of St. Severin at Heiligenstadt near Vienna, cf. the Excursus, pp. 112ff.
97 44.1-3.
98 44.5-7.
99 It is on this occasion that Eugippius gives the only detail of Severin's exterior, viz. that he wore a beard.
100 46.1, 2.
101 46.6.
102 3.1; 9.181; 11.19.
103 Ch. 4 (MGH Scriptores 15.1, 1887, p. 102, 12).
104 AS Januarii tom. 1. 734-739. (Bibl. hagiogr. Lat. nr. 7658.)

were taken to the suburb of Fratta Maggiore.[105] A testimony to the cult of St. Severin is also the hymn on his feast day, which is presented on pp. 104-9, of this volume.[106]

---

[105] Robinson, p. 107-109, with references; Winter, KW 2.200-203.
[106] This hymn is preserved in two eleventh-century MSS, Vatic. 7172, and Paris. Lat. 1092. It was edited from the Vatican MS by Knoell, p. 71ff., and Mommsen, p. viiif., and from both MSS by G. M. Dreves, *Analecta Hymnica Medii Aevi* 14 a (1893), 47f. W. Bulst prints the Vatican text with an apparatus of scholarly emendations, *Editiones Heidelbergenses* 10, p. 54f.

III. THE CHURCH OF NORICUM IN THE TIME OF
SAINT SEVERIN[1]

UGIPPIUS' REFERENCES to the ecclesiastical conditions of Noricum are so frequent and so detailed that they deserve to be discussed more fully than has been done in the preceding chapters.
The existence of church buildings in all towns of Noricum and Raetia visited by Severin is either expressly mentioned or implied; the latter for Ioviaco, by the presence of a resident priest,[2] and for Tiburnia, as an episcopal see.[3] Eugippius distinguishes between *ecclesia* and *basilica*.[4] The *ecclesia* is always a public church.[5] It should be noted that all of Eugippius' *ecclesiae* are found in the smaller towns; at Lauriacum, which was the see of a bishop, the distribution of oil takes place in a *basilica*.[6] The word *basilica* is, however, used also for a monastic church, for example, for those at Favianis,[7] Boiotro,[8] and Iuvao.[9] Sometimes, the church of a small town is found outside its walls, as in Quintanis, probably for lack of building space. This church is interesting also architecturally; it was built of wood, not of stone, and it was a 'sus-

---

1 Cf. Noll, *Christentum*, pp. 121-124.
2 24.2.
3 21.2.
4 The word *oratorium* does not denote a church, but a room for private prayer, e.g., Severin's cell, 39.1.
5 1.1 (Asturis); 1.4 (Comagenis); 11.2 (Cucullis); 15.1 (Quintanis).
6 29.2.
7 9.3; 10.1.
8 22.1.
9 13.1. That this is a monastic church may be concluded from the reference, in 14.1, to Severin's *cellula*.

pension structure,' supported by posts with forked tops.[10] Public churches had a baptistery, a sexagonal or octagonal building beside the main one.[11] Eugippius mentions the baptistery of Batavis.[12]

Since the fourth century, the altarstones over which Mass was said normally held relics of martyrs. It was obviously for this purpose that Severin collected relics (*sanctuaria, benedictio*)[13] for his monastery at Favianis, viz. those of the martyrs, Gervasius and Protasius[14] and of St. John the Baptist.[15] The demand for relics was already great enough to encourage the circulation of false ones; but Severin was always assured by a previous revelation[16] that the relics which he obtained were genuine.

The churches were furnished with silver vessels, especially silver chalices, which often aroused the greed of plunderers.[17] Lights were kindled for services.[18] The clergy and laity, it seems, assembled in separate parts of the church,[19] which were divided by barriers.[20]

On the subject of religious services, Eugippius is less explicit than one might wish. On several occasions, he speaks

---

10 It does not follow from Eugippius' words that this church was erected over the river (so Sommerlad, p. 35ff., Robinson, p. 60). The words 15.3 *ipse subter navi* (navim TMS) *descendens* most probably mean that Severin descended underneath the aisle of the church; in late Latin, the distinction between accusative and ablative tends to disappear, especially after prepositions.
11 Cf. the plan of the baptistery at Ivenna on the Drave, Zeiller, p. 183, and the description of the baptistery excavated at Carnuntum, Noll, p. 196; Noll, *Christentum*, p. 130 and pl. 7.
12 22.3; 5. It was not at Boiotro, a place outside Batavis mentioned in 22.1; with 22.2, we are back to the city.
13 Cf. Paulinus of Nola, Epist. 32.8, who refers to a particle of the Cross as *hanc de cruce benedictionem*. The destination of the relics, viz. to be enclosed in altarstones, seems indicated in the phrase *collocavit* (*sacravit*) *officio sacerdotum*, 9.3; 23.2.
14 9.2, 3.
15 22.1; ch. 23.
16 9.3.
17 Cf. 44.1.
18 13.1.
19 12.3 *unusquisque in ordine suo psallebat*—or does this simply mean 'each in his turn'?
20 *Saepta*, 16.2.

of *vespertinum sacrificium*,[21] or *sacrificium vespertini temporis*;[22] the same service is understood in 12.3, where the poor man of Cucullis leaves the congregation which has assembled in the morning, and returns to the church in the evening *communicaturus* (most probably 'in order to communicate'), and in 11.3, where 'after the customary singing of psalms' *ad horam sacrificii,* Severin works the miracle of the tapers. Sommerlad interprets these passages—correctly, it seems—as references to Evening Mass. This does not mean that in fifth-century Noricum Mass was normally said in the evening. However, it had been the practice of the Western Church since the end of the fourth century to celebrate the Eucharist in the evening *(ad nonam horam)* [23] on Saturdays and days of fast.[24] It should be noted that in 2.1 and 11.3, the 'sacrifice' is celebrated at the end of a three days' fast; the same seems to be implied in 12.2. The expression *vespertinum sacrificium,* it would appear, had become technical; even at its first recorded occurrence,[25] it is clearly related to the celebration of the Eucharist. Evening Mass was preceded by the singing of psalms, which was an established custom,[26] and not only on days when it was followed by the Eucharastic sacrifice.[27]

The only other service mentioned in our text is the vigil of the dead. The deceased priest, Silvinus of Quintanis, is laid out on a bier in church, and people and clergy[28] sing pslams

---

[21] 2.1.
[22] 13.2; called also *vespertina sollemnitas,* 13.1.
[23] This evidently is the hour understood by Eugippius, 11.3 *ad horam sacrificii;* 13.1 *tempus vespertini sollemnitatis.*
[24] Dom E. Dekkers. *L'église ancienne a-t-elle connu la messe du soir?* in *Miscellanea Liturgica in honorem L. Cunibert Mohlberg,* 1 (Bibliotheca 'Ephemerides Liturgicae' 22, Rome 1948) 231-257; cf. *Sacris Erudiri* 7 (1955) 99-130.
[25] St. Ambrose, *Commentary on the 118th Psalm,* 8.48 (ed. M. Petschenig, CSEL 62 [Vienna 1913] 180, line 17f.).
[26] *Ex more,* 11.3; 12.3.
[27] Cf. 30.3; of Severin's monks, 39.1; 44.5.
[28] Also, it would appear, the clergy from neighboring places. Severin bids 'all the priests and deacons to retire for rest' and remains 'only with the priest and deacon and the two janitors,' obviously the clergy of Quintanis: 16.1,3.

all the night through. A similar service was held on the anniversary of a priest's or cleric's death. Lucillus thus celebrates the anniversary of his former abbot, the late bishop Valentinus,[29] and Severin foretells him that his own vigil will have to be held on the same day.[30] From the description of Severin's first (provisional) burial, it may be inferred that a body was normally wrapped in linen and so buried; it was not customary either to embalm the body or to enclose it in a coffin.[31] It is only in view of future emigration (prophesied by the saint!) that *after his burial*[32] a coffin is made and kept in readiness. Strangely interesting is the custom, referred to incidentally, of preparing the funeral at a time when the dying person was still alive.[33]

Twice Severin is reported to have used a formula of blessing, *viz. Sit nomen Domini benedictum*. This blessing he pronounces before the distribution of oil to the poor at Lauriacum[34]—with the effect that the oil is miraculously increased—and as a short prayer of thanksgiving for the miraculous rescue of the Noricans who crossed the Alps in mid-winter.[35]

Among other religious observances, we hear a great deal about fasts.[36] A special fast prescribed for the whole congregation would normally last three days;[37] special fasts of forty days were observed in monasteries.[38]

Of greater interest to the historian is Eugippius' testimony regarding ecclesiastical organization. We find a fully developed ecclesiastical hierarchy, from the bishop down to the *ostiarius*.

---

29 41.1.
30 It is not certain that the custom was universal. All the instances recorded concern persons who were either in religion or in Holy Orders.
31 44.6.
32 43.9.
33 14.1; 33.1.
34 28.3.
35 29.4.
36 Cf. above, pp. 29; 35.
37 2.1; 11.1; 25.2.
38 Ch. 36; 38.

The metropolitan[39] of all Noricum had his see at Tiburnia, which, as ecclesiastical metropolis,[40] had succeeded Sirmium, then destroyed by the Huns. Paulinus, who was elected bishop of Tiburnia, is said to hold *summi sacerdotii principatum,* that is, as Zibermayr[41] explains, the first place among the bishops of Noricum. The metropolitan of Noricum Ripense resided at Lauriacum.[42] According to Zibermayr's plausible argumentation, there was also a suffragan at Favianis; it was this dignity that fell to the former tribune, Mamertinus, after the refusal of Severin.[43] The three sees, therefore, coincide with the capitals of Noricum, Noricum Ripense, and the lower district of the latter *(regio inferior),* respectively. Ecclesiastical organization follows in the footsteps of civil administration.

We also learn about a bishop Valentinus of Raetia, who at some time was abbot of a monastery.[44]

The bishop was then, as in earlier times, elected by popular acclamation.[45]

Priests and deacons are found in every town. Even such a small place as Cucullis seems to have had several.[46] Quintanis,[47] another small town, had one priest (beside the recently deceased Silvinus), one deacon, a subdeacon named Marcus,[48] and two persons of minor rank who are styled

---

39 This whole paragraph is based on Zibermayr, pp. 46-51; differently, Noll², p. 138.
40 It is so called expressly in 21.2.
41 P. 50.
42 He is called *pontifex* by Eugippius (30.2) and Ennodius *(Vita s. Antonii* 14); Lauriacum alone among all Norican towns is termed *urbs. Pontifex* denoted the chief priest of a province in Christian times as it had in the days of paganism; Ovilava, the former capital of Noricum used to have a *pontifex*: CIL 3.1 (1873), nr. 5630.
43 4.2; cf. Zibermayr, p. 49.
44 41.1.
45 21.2.
46 Eugippius consistently uses the plural: 11.2,3; 12.1.
47 Ch. 16.
48 However, the MSS of Mommsen's Class II read *diaconi.*

ianitores, viz. the *ostiarius* Maternus,[49] and an *aedituus*.[50] A *cantor* ('Chanter'), Moderatus, is mentioned in 24.1; he apparently belonged to the Church of Batavis. How far church choirs may have developed in Noricum we do not know; it is only from Italy that we hear about a *primicerius cantorum*.[51] Significantly, all members of the Norican clergy have Roman names.

The priests, and par excellence the bishops, enjoyed a privileged social position; Eugippius always singles them out from the rest of the population.[52] In the absence of an efficient civil government, the bishop is also the supreme authority in civil affairs; hence, Severin at Lauriacum gives a message of a purely secular nature to bishop Constantius 'and the others who were there.'[53]

There were a number of priests among Severin's monks.[54] Two of these we know by name, *viz.* Lucillus[55] and Marcianus,[56] who, in turn, succeeded Severin as head of his monastic foundation before Eugippius. There is no reason for

---

49 16.2; cf. 16.6.
50 The former was probably in Holy Orders, but not so the latter; cf. *Maurus basilicae monasterii . . . aedituus*, 10. 1 (in the *Capitula*, he is styled *ostiarius*). *Aedituus* is the 'sacristan' or 'clerk' of the church (Zeiller, p. 178); the same office is apparently referred to in 1.3, where Eugippius speaks of *ecclesiae custos*. The duties assigned to the *custodes sacrarii* according to Isidore of Seville (*De officiis ecclesiasticis* 2.9; *Regula monachorum* 20) correspond exactly to those of a sacristan. The *ministri* of 29.3 would seem to be 'altar boys.'
51 *Marinus primicerius cantorum sanctae ecclesiae Neapolitanae*, 46.5. *Primicerius* is the person whose name heads the staff roll (*cera*, because it was a waxen tablet), hence, 'head of a government department,' e.g., *primicerius notariorum* 'chief secretary,' 'chancellor.' The title *primicerius cantorum* (recorded only from this passage) suggests that, at least, the more important churches in Italy had permanent and well-organized church choirs. Is the *primicerius cantorum* the 'choirmaster'?
52 Cf. Epist. Eugipp. 7 *sacerdotes et spiritales viri nec non et laici nobiles atque religiosi*; Commemoratorium 1.2 *presbyteris, clero vel civibus*; 12.1 *presbyteri ceterique mansores*.
53 30.2.
54 9.3; 22.1; 23.2.
55 19.5; 41.1; 44.5; 45.2.
56 11.2; 37.1; 46.1.

THE LIFE OF SAINT SEVERIN 45

assuming (as did Schuster)[57] that Eugippius styles them *presbyter* with reference to their monastic authority.

Beside persons in Holy Orders, there were others of a distinct religious status. There are, first of all, those of Severin's monks who were not ordained. At Quintanis, a *virgo consecrata* hides in the Church, hoping to witness a miracle;[58]

---

57 P. 176. The term *presbyter* may be accepted in the *Commemoratorium* in the sense of 'priest': (a) when it is taken up by *sacerdos* with reference to the same person: Primenius, Epist. Eugipp. 8 and 10, cf. 9; the presbyter of Batavis, 22.3, cf. 5; or (b) when it is found in conjunction with other terms indicative of ecclesiastical rank: 11.2; 16.4ff.; 1.2 (*presbyteris, clero vel civibus*, cf. Epist. Eugipp. 7 *sacerdotes, spiritales viri, laici nobiles*); or (c) where mention is made of the presbyter(s) of a particular locality: 11.2 (Severin prescribes a fast at Cucullis *per presbyteros loci*); 16.1 (Silvinus of Quintanis, *castelli presbyter*); 22.1 (the presbyter of the basilica at Boiotro—Batavis, cf. 22.3 and 5); in all probability also the presbyter Maximianus of Ioviaco, *spiritalis vitae presbyter*, 24.2 (apparently not a monk, but a secular priest who privately lived according to the counsels of perfection). Two monks of St. Severin, who are styled *presbyter noster*, Lucillus and Marcianus, were both abbots of the community: Lucillus at the time of the transmigration from Noricum to Italy (44.5), Marcianus at the time of the *translatio* of the saint's body to Lucullanum (46.1). The wording of these passages (*venerabilis noster pater tunc Lucillus*; Barbara *venerabilem patrem nostrum Marcianum, sed et cunctam congregationem . . . invitavit*, cf. 37.1 *Marcianus monachus, qui postea presbyter ante nos monasterio praefuit*, and, possibly in the same sense, 11.2 *Marciani, post presbyteri nostri*) might suggest that presbyter both times means 'abbot,' and the same might, then, be presumed for Eugippius himself, where he is styled *presbyter* (Epist. Pasch., title, and in the letters addressed to him, cf. p. 3, n. 3). However, Lucillus is termed *sanctus presbyter* both before and after Severin's death (19.5: 41.1; 45.2), and the meaning of the word in those passages is hardly that of *senior*, a term not unknown to Eugippius (*seniores nostri*, 43.9; cf. *maiorum relatione*, Epist. Eugipp. 2). Severin himself addresses Lucillus *sancte presbyter* (41.2), similarly he addresses Paulinus, later to become a bishop, *venerabilis presbyter* (21.1)—which, in the monastic sense of 'elder,' would be rather inappropriate for the head of a community (elsewhere Severin refers to a priest as *sacerdos*: Primenius, Epist. Eugipp. 9; the presbyter of Batavis, 22.5). There remains the presbyter to whom the *epistola de vita Bassi* was addressed (Epist. Eugipp. 1). His status is as unknown to us as is his person; the presumption, in the light of Eugippius' usage, is that he was a priest. As regards Eugippius himself, it seems to us that the 'style' of Paschasius' address: *Domino sancto semperque carissimo Eugippio presbytero Paschasius diaconus* is suggestive of Eugippius having been a priest, cf. our (b)-cases above, and so is the address of the letter written to him by Fulgentius of Ruspe: *Domino beatissimo . . . sancto fratri et conpresbytero Eugyppio*.
58 16.2.

Eugippius' words are best understood as meaning that this lady has taken a personal vow of virginity.[59] There are further several references to certain persons as *religiosi* and *spiritales*, but the distinction between them is not quite clear.[60]

Finally, attention must be called to a particular form of religious expression which is as strange to us as it was common in Severin's days—the shedding of tears. Tears of repentance are shed, not only by Queen Giso[61] and by the poor man of Cucullis,[62] whose behavior is understandable in the situation, but also by the people of Comagenis at large who atone for their former obstinacy to Severin's warnings.[63] When Severin advises his monks to drown their sensual urges in holy tears,[64] his advice is meant quite literally. Severin himself professes with tears his own unworthiness;[65] his praying with tears is reported especially before a miraculous cure.[66] In classical antiquity, we should remember, even men were not ashamed of tears;[67] of the Latins, this is true to the present day.

---

59 Noll, p. 168.
60 The *viri religiosi* Epist. Eugipp. 1, seem to be persons in religion, but not so the *laici nobiles et religiosi*, ibid. 8, who are contrasted with the *spiritales viri*; the latter are probably monks (not necessarily priests, 'Klostergeistliche,' as suggested by Noll, p. 166), cf. also 13.2 *in conspectu trium spiritalium . . . virorum*, and Severin as *spiritalis doctor*, 39.1. The priest, Maximianus, *spiritalis vitae* (24.2) was not a monk, but probably observed certain monastic devotions and ascetic practices. All those who are not monks, clergy and laity alike, are termed *saeculares* (10.1; 43.6).
61 8.4.
62 12.6.
63 2.1.
64 9.5; cf. 34.1; 43.5.
65 14.2.
66 14.3; 16.4.
67 Noll, p. 39.

TO THE HOLY AND VENERABLE LORD, THE DEACON PASCHASIUS,[1] EUGIPPIUS (SENDS) A GREETING IN CHRIST

ABOUT TWO YEARS AGO, during the consulate of Inportunus, we had the privilege to read a letter of some noble layman to a priest; it contained the life of the monk, Bassus, who at one time lived in the monastery of the so-called Mount Titas above Ariminum, and later died in the district of Lucania—a man well known to me as to many others. When I learnt that of this letter some people took copies, I began to think by myself, and also tell persons in religion, that it was not right to conceal the great miracles which the power of God had worked through the blessed Severin.[2]

(2) Of this the author of that letter came to know. The idea appealed to him, and he asked me to send him for his information some sketches concerning this holy Severin so that he could write a little book about his life for the benefit of posterity. Prompted by this offer, I drafted a memorandum; it comprised a number of sketches based on stories that are familiar to us from the daily accounts of our elders. Yet I was far from feeling happy about it. It was not justifiable, I thought, that in your lifetime we should ask a layman to undertake this work. There even seemed to be some risk in entrusting a lay writer with a work of this type and style. A man trained, for all that we know, only in secular literature would probably

---
1 Details about persons and places mentioned by Eugippius will be found in the special index at the end of the text, p. 123ff.
2 The attributes 'blessed' (*beatus*) or 'holy' (*sanctus*) are, in Christian antiquity, frequently given to living persons who had a reputation for saintliness.

write that Life in a style far too difficult for the majority of unlearned people, and the splendor of wonderful things which have long been hidden, as it were, under a night of silence might now—as far as we, the uneducated,[3] are concerned—be veiled by the obscurities of eloquence. (3) However this may be, I am not going to look out for the fickle flame of that lamp as long as you shine like the sun; only, do not allow the cloud of some excuse to stand before the rays of your knowledge—I mean, by pleading your own incompetence. Please, do not strike me with harsh words, saying: 'Why do you hope for water out of a stone?' Indeed, I do not expect it from the stone of the worldly road, but from you, who, comparing spiritual things with spiritual,[4] will refresh us, out of a solid rock, with the honey[5] of speech that flows from your mouth. Of this, even now, you give us the nectar-like forestate of a sweet promise: you demand that I should send you my memorandum or sketches concerning the life of the oft-mentioned St. Severin. Let us then hope that, until they have been transformed into a book of your composition, they will not offend any critic. (4) For everyone who wants an architect to build a house prepares carefully the necessary building materials; if, however, the craftsman does not turn up in time, and our man puts up a wall resembling a pier of unhewn stone, can he be said to have been building—in the absence of any professional construction, without even the proper laying of a safe foundation? So it is with me. Just barely preparing precious material for your great art, can I, with my humble style, be thought to have written what I would like to write—without the professional skill of an educated writer, without the trimmings of stylistic elegance?

(5) The one sure foundation which my writing has is that

---

3 *Ignaros liberalium litterarum*. Eugippius means to imply that he has not been trained in the highly rhetorical style of writing which was then the fashion. He must not be taken too literally, cf. Introduction, p. 6f.
4 Cf. 1 Cor. 2.13.
5 *De petra . . . melle*: cf. Deut. 32.13.

faith by which the holy man excelled in deeds of wonder. This, here, I now hand over to you so that it may be shaped by your tongue and, when your work has been completed, I shall give thanks to Christ as is His due.

(6) Let me mention also, I pray, the wonderful graces and miraculous cures the power of God has worked, either on the way or here[6] at the tomb of this our blessed father. Since the faithful bearer of this message, your son, Deogratias,[7] knows them well, we have left it to him to make them known to you by word of mouth. We also hope to have ample opportunity of uttering the bearer's name[8] when your work is finished, so that the loyal servant of God, having attained to the glory of the saints by his good deeds through the grace of Christ, may, by your written word, be known as a saint also to the memory of men.

(7) Perhaps we are obliged to ask the question from which country he came since it is customary for a biographer to take this as his start. Yet I must confess that I have no certain information on this point. (8) Many priests and spiritual men, but also noble and religious laymen, natives as well as others who came to him from far away, guessed and asked each other to what nation the man belonged who worked such great miracles before their eyes, but nobody dared to ask him openly; at last, a certain Primenius, a noble priest of Italy, and a man who commanded every possible authority—he had sought the saint's protection at the time when the patrician, Orestes, had been unjustly killed, for fear of Orestes' murderers, because he had been to him as a father—after many days of intimate friendship burst out, as in the name of them all, with the question, saying: 'Holy master, what is the

---
6 In the monastery of Castellum Lucullanum, where Eugippius writes.
7 The names Deogratias, Deogratia, are found also in Christian inscriptions. Cf. E. Diehl, *Inscriptiones Latinae Christianae* 3 (1931) 47. Names of this type were common at that time; Schuster, p. 195, refers to St. Augustine's son, Adeodatus, and to the African bishop, Quodvultdeus.
8 That is, of saying 'Deo gratias.' A pious pun. So already Mommsen, *Gesammelte Schriften* 7 (1909) 523f.

province from which God has deigned to send such a great light as His gift to these districts?' (9) The man of God first replied in joke: 'If you think I am a runaway slave have money ready to offer for me when I am claimed.' But then, turning serious, he added something like this: 'What good does it do a servant of God to make known his birthplace or family? By keeping silence about it, he can more easily avoid pride, which is on his left side; without letting his left hand know,[9] he wishes to perform every good work by the grace of Christ, and thus to be made worthy of the company of those who stand on His right side,[10] and to be enlisted as a citizen of the heavenly fatherland. If you realize that I, though I am unworthy, strive for this, why must you know my country on earth, for which you ask? This, however, you should know: that God, who has made you a priest, has also ordered me to come to these people in their hour of need.' (10) By this reply, the priest was silenced, and nobody else, either before or after this, ever dared to ask the holy man a similar question. His language, however, proved him a true Latin. Earlier in his life, as is known for certain, he had gone to some desert in the east, burning with desire for a more perfect life; afterwards, compelled by divine revelation, he had left there and gone to the towns of Noricum Ripense, bordering on Upper Pannonia, towns which were afflicted by frequent raids of the barbarians. This he used to indicate in veiled language, as if he were speaking of somebody else, mentioning by name some cities of the east and hinting at the dangers of the endless journey which he had miraculously overcome. What I have told here is all that I have ever heard when our conversation turned on blessed Severin's home—even in his lifetime. (11) The sketches, then, of his miraculous life are drafted in the *Memorandum* which, with its summary of chapters prefixed, follows upon this letter. They will, as is my request, gain in fame by a book from your

---
9 Matt. 6.3.
10 Matt. 25.33.

masterly pen. It remains for me to ask that you may never cease to unite your prayers with his and to obtain for me God's pardon.

CHAPTERS[11]

1. How Severin first came to be known in a town named Asturis by a wholesome exhortation to good works and by a true prophecy.

2. Of a town named Comagenis, which he miraculously freed from the enemy.

3. That through his prayer, God came to the help of the inhabitants of the small town of Favianis who suffered from famine.

4. Of the barbarian robbers who lost all their arms, together with their booty which they had taken outside the walls of Favianis; and of his way of life and his extraordinary humility.

5. In what great respect he was held by the king of the Rugi, Flaccitheus, and how, by Severin's foretelling, the king escaped an ambush of his enemies.

6. Of the only son of a widow of the said people of the Rugi, who was tormented by pain for twelve years, and was healed by the prayer of the man of God.

---

11 According to Epist. Eugipp. 11 (*praelatis capitulis*), these chapter headings are the work of Eugippius. However, in ch. 36 we read: 'Of this action, quoting the examples of two of the fathers, he has given a most truthful justification in the proper place.' For 'he has given' (*reddidit*) MSS TN read *reddidi* 'I have given.' If, as it seems, the third person is the genuine reading, the subject of 'has given' must be Eugippius, not Severin; it is the author who, by way of justifying Severin's action, quotes the examples of St. Ambrose and Postumianus. The chapter headings were then added by some later editor. Cf. *Capitula in Matthaeum* 28 (D Ep G K Q) *nomina apostolorum dicit* (the Evangelist) *quos missit* (Christ) *cum omni doctrina*. There are other discrepancies between these headings and the text. In heading 10, Maurus is referred to as *ostiarius*; in the text, he is styled *aedituus* (cf. above, p. 44 with n. 50). Heading 13 speaks of *vespertinae laudis officium* ('vespers'), whereas the text suggests evening mass (cf. above, p. 40f.). It would follow that the words 'with its summary of chapters prefixed' were inserted in Epist. Eugipp. 11 bʸ the redactor of this table of contents.

7. How young Odovacar, clad in mean hides, was told by him that he was going to be king.

8. That Feletheus, also named Feva, king of the Rugi, and son of the said Flaccitheus, for fear of St. Severin, forbade his wicked wife to rebaptize Catholics; and what danger befell her little son, Fredericus, one day when she had spurned the saint's intercession for certain persons.

9. Of the bearer of relics of St. Gervasius and St. Protasius, the martyrs, who was made known by a miraculous revelation of the man of God; and what was his answer when he declined the honor of being made bishop.

10. Of an usher who, on a certain day, was forbidden to go out anywhere; who was captured by the barbarians and humbly brought back by them.

11. Of a miracle worked in the castle of Cucullis, where, through tapers lighted by divine power, sacrilegious persons who had first concealed themselves were made known and amended.

12. How locusts were expelled from the lands of the said castle after God had been propitiated by fast, prayer, and alms; and how the corn of one poor man was eaten up because he did not believe and scorned the saint.

13. How a candle which the servant of God held in his hand at prayer was kindled when, at the time of the evening service of praise, the fire required by custom was not found.

14. Of the miraculous healing of a woman that was given up, who, after a long and agonizing sickness, recovered so quickly through the prayer of the man of God that on the third day she was strong enough to take up work in the fields.

15. How in the posts sustaining the river-side of a church which the floods often covered, the servant of God, saying a prayer, incised the sign of the cross with an axe—a sign above which the water after this never rose.

16. Of the deceased priest, Silvinus, whose dead body, lying on the bier during the night vigil, suddenly, when the saint called him, opened his eyes, and who asked the servant of

God, at whose call he had come to life, not to deprive him further of the rest which he had tasted.

17. With what anxious care he looked after the poor, and that the Norici used to send him tithes for distribution, and that when these were brought to him according to custom, he foretold danger for those who had delayed to send them.

18. How the rust which had appeared and threatened the crops was removed through the man of God by fasts and prayers.

19. That Gibuld, king of the Alamanni, was shaken with great trembling in the presence of the man of God, and restored a great number of captives.

20. How it was revealed to him that soldiers had been killed, and how he directed his people, who knew nothing, to the river in order to bury the bodies.

21. When the priest, Paulinus, who had come to him from afar, was going back to his home, Severin foretold that he was soon to be ordained bishop of Noricum.

22. That when holy relics were being sought for a new basilica, he foretold that he would be offered the blessing of St. John the Baptist without asking, and that in that town during his absence, there would be a massacre in which a priest who had used bad language would be killed.

23. How he received the said holy relics.

24. Of the inhabitants of another town who did not care for his prophetic command, and who were soon afterwards killed by the Heruli because, in spite of his warning, they would not leave the place.

25. How in letters directed to Noricum, he fortified the strongholds with fasts and almsgiving so that the raid of the enemies he had predicted could do them no harm.

26. Of the healed leper, who, for fear of contracting the leprosy of sin, declined to go home.

27. Of the victory which the Romans won over the Alamanni at Batavis through the prayer of St. Severin, and, that after the triumph, those who refused to follow him when he prophetically warned them were killed.

28. How it happened that when the servant of God ministered to the poor the oil increased.

29. Of those men who carried on their shoulders clothing from Noricum to be given to the poor, for whom, in the middle of winter, a bear led the way through a solitude of snow to human dwellings, and how the man of God, by his familiar gift of foreknowledge, knew that they had such a guide on their way.

30. How he knew beforehand that, in the following night, the enemy would come against the city of Lauriacum, and how with difficulty he persuaded the citizens, lulled in false security, to keep a watch; and how, in the morning, after they had found him to be right, they asked forgiveness of their unbelief and thanked him.

31. How, when Feva, king of the Rugi, came with his army to Lauriacum, Severin went out to meet him, and how the king received the population into his protection in order to evacuate them to towns further down (the Danube), that is, nearer to the Rugi.

32. How king Odovacar requested that he should ask him a favor, and how, at the written word of the servant of God, he recalled a certain Ambrosius from exile, and how the same servant of God foretold the king's flatterers how many years he would reign.

33. Of the son of one of the nobles of the king of the Rugi in the town of Comagenis, who was healed by the prayer of the man of God.

34. How a leper named Teio was healed.

35. Of the monk, Bonosus, who, when complaining about his poor eyesight, was told by him: 'Rather pray to see more with your heart'; soon afterwards he was deigned to receive miraculously the gift of prolonged prayer.

36. Of three proud monks, whom he delivered to Satan in order that their spirits might be saved. Of this action (the author), quoting the examples of two of the fathers, has given a most truthful justification in the proper place.

37. How he signified the hour of tribulation of his monks, Marcianus and Renatus, which they had to endure while in another province, and how he urged the other brethren, who were present, to pray for them.

38. Of the danger of a deadly pustule, which he by revelation foretold the monk, Ursus, forty days in advance and which he healed by prayer.

39. A few things are briefly indicated about the blessed man's dwelling, his bed, and his food.

40. How, when by divine revelation he felt his departure to be near, he talked to king Feva and his wicked queen, and how, after that, he never ceased to prepare his followers for the coming events, foretelling them the emigration of the whole populace, and demanding that they should take his body along.

41. How to the holy priest, Lucillus, he signified clearly even the day of his death.

42. How he adjured Ferderuchus, son of the said king Feva, and advised his own people.

43. Of his death and of the advice which he gave his followers in a long, last exhortation.

44. What Ferderuchus did to his monastery after his decease and how he was punished, and how his prophecy was fulfilled by the prosperous migration of the people, and how his body was disinterred and put on a wagon.

45. Of the healing of many sick persons on that occasion. Leaving aside other details, only the words of a mute person are reported which he uttered in prayer under the wagon when the body was still on it.

46. Of the faith of the noble lady, Barbaria, who received the body on her estate, and how the people of Naples went out to meet the body. Whilst on this occasion many were healed of various diseases, only three cases of healing are recorded.

MEMORANDUM

1 (1) At the time when Attila, king of the Huns, had died, the two Pannonias and the other districts bordering on the Danube were in a state of utter confusion. It was then that the most holy servant of God, Severin, who had come from the eastern parts to the borderland of Noricum Ripense and the Pannonias, stayed in a small town called Asturis. By a life according to the precepts of the Gospel and the apostles, a model of piety and chastity,[1] he gave proof of his Catholic faith, living up, as he did, to his venerable ideal by holy works. (2) Whilst, strengthened by such practice, he strove in innocence for the heavenly palm, one day, as he was used to do, he went to the church. He asked the priests, the clergy, and the layfolk to be called together, and then, in all the humbleness of his mind, foretold them how, with prayer, fasting, and fruits of mercy, they might prevent the imminent attack of the enemy. But they, proud as they were and defiled by the desires of the flesh, judged the warnings of the prophet by the standard of their unbelief. (3) The servant of God, however, returned to his abode, where he had found hospitality with the sacristan of the church; he revealed the day and hour of the impending disaster and said: 'I hasten to leave a stubborn city which will soon perish' Then he turned away[2] to a neighbor-

453

---

1 1 Tim. 2.2.
2 *Ad proximum . . . oppidum declinavit.* '*Declinavit* alludes to a diversion from an intended route; this fact might have some bearing on the localization of Favianis': KW 1.116. The implication is this, that Severin, having arrived at Asturis (by boat), had planned to go to Favianis (supposed by the authors to be Heiligenstadt near Vienna) from there, but changed his route when he saw the fall of Asturis. There is nothing in Eugippius to suggest, (a) Severin's traveling from the East to Asturis on the Danube; (b) a plan on his part of going to Favianis from there directly; (c) a subsequent change of route. Severin

ing town, which was called Comagenis. (4) This town was held in strict occupation by a troop of barbarians inside, who had concluded a treaty with the Romans, and nobody would easily be given permission either to leave or to enter. And yet the man of God, unknown though he was, passed unquestioned and unimpeded. He went to the church at once, and urged the whole population, which had already given up all hope, to arm themselves with fast, prayer, and almsgiving; he held up to them the ancient examples of salvation from danger when the protection of God had miraculously freed His people contrary to all expectation. (5) They hesitated to believe the man who, at the very moment of the emergency, promised them all their safety when an old man, who had formerly received the noble guest in Asturis, arrived and, anxiously questioned by the guards at the gates, proved by his outward appearance as well as by his words the destruction of his town; he added that the town had been destroyed by the barbarians the very same day which the man of God had foretold. When they heard this, they eagerly replied: 'Is this not the very same man who, in our utter despair, promises us the assistance of God?' The old man at once recognized in the church the servant of God; he threw himself to his feet and declared that it was by this man's merit that he escaped and was not caught by the disaster as were all his fellow citizens.

2 (1) When the inhabitants of the said city heard this, they begged pardon for their unbelief, carried out the holy works which the man of God had urged, observed fasts, and, gathering in the church for three days, made up for their past faults with sighs and tears. On the third day, when the evening sacrifice was being celebrated, there suddenly started an earthquake. By this, the barbarians in the town were so terrified that they forced the Romans to open the gates for them with-

---

had, for the time being, settled down in Asturis (1.1). Only when he foresaw that the town was doomed because its inhabitants would not listen to his exhortations (1.2), he 'turned away.' The verb *declinavit* takes up *abscedo* in the saint's own words immediately preceding.

out delay. (2) Swarming out in a hurry in every direction—they imagined that they were encircled and besieged by their hostile neighbors, and their terror was still increased by the power of God—and straying in the dark of night, they killed each other with their swords. The people, freed through God's aid by this mutual destruction of their enemies, learnt from the holy man to fight with heavenly arms.

3 (1) At the same time, a city named Favianis had been befallen by cruel famine, and its inhabitants believed that their sole remedy was to invite, with pious solicitations, the man of God from the said town of Comagenis. The Lord made him know beforehand that they would come to him and bade him go with them. When he had come there, he advised the townspeople, saying: (2) 'By the fruits of penance you can be freed from the great calamity of this famine.' Whilst they were striving to do as they had been told, blessed Severin learnt by divine revelation that a widow named Procula had hidden great quantities of grain. He made her come forward in front of all and vehemently reproached her. 'Why,' he said, 'do you, daughter of a noble family, make yourself a servant to greed, and a slave to avarice, which, as the Apostle teaches, is idolatry?[3] Look here, whilst the Lord provides mercifully for his servants you will not be able to do anything with your ill-gotten gains except that you may throw into the water of the Danube the grain which you have withheld so long and show the fishes a kindness which you have denied to your fellowmen. Therefore, help yourself rather than the poor with the goods which so far you have decided to hold back whilst Christ goes hungry.'[4] The woman, struck with fear by these words, began to give ungrudgingly to the poor what she had amassed. (3) Not long after, one could see on the shore of the Danube many boats from Raetia, full of goods, which had been held up for many days by the heavy ice of the river Inn. Now, by the command of God, the ice had broken and the

---
3 Eph. 5.5.
4 Cf. Matt. 25.42.

boats brought lots of food to the people who were suffering from famine. Then they all, with unceasing devotion, praised God who had granted them such unforeseen help, for they had been expecting to fade away by this long famine, and they declared that, beyond a doubt, it was through the prayers of the servant of God that the boats were freed, out of season, from the wintry ice.

4 (1) About the same time, a band of barbarians made a sudden incursion and whatever they could find outside the walls, be it people or cattle, they dragged away. A number of the citizens, then, with tears gathered round the man of God and related the sad losses they had suffered; they also showed him evidence of the recent robbery. (2) He, in turn, asked Mamertinus, who was at that time tribune and afterwards was consecrated bishop, whether he had at his disposal some men in arms with whom he could chase the robbers effectively. He answered: 'Soldiers I have—just a few—but with these I dare not attack such a host of enemies. If, however, Your Worship so commands, we believe, although lacking the necessary supply of arms, yet to win a victory by your prayer.' (3) And the servant of God said: 'Although your soldiers have no arms, they will now get their arms from the enemy. Neither numbers nor human courage is required when God clearly proves Himself our champion. Just go in the name of the Lord; go fast, go with confidence. Led mercifully by God, even the greatest coward will appear a hero. "The Lord will fight for you,"[5] and you will be silent. Go, therefore, without delay, but observe this one command above all: any of the barbarians whom you may take prisoner you must bring to me unharmed.' (4) So they go out, and at the second milestone, on a brook called Tiguntia, they find the said robbers. The soldiers at once turned them to flight, seized the arms of all, and made some prisoners; these they bound and, as they had been told, brought them before the servant of God. He set them free, gave them to eat and to drink, and

---

5 Exod. 14.14.

then briefly addressed them: 'Go and tell your accomplices not to dare and come here again, greedy for plunder. They will be punished at once by a sentence of heavenly vengeance. God fights for His servants, and the power from above always protects them so strongly that, not only can the weapons of the enemy inflict no wounds upon them, but the enemy himself provides them with arms.' (5) He then let the barbarians go, and for himself rejoiced in the miracles of Christ, and further promised that by His mercy that town would never in the future experience looting by an enemy; only its inhabitants should never let themselves be deterred from the work of God by either good or bad fortune.

(6) Then blessed Severin retreated to an out-of-the-way place, called 'At the Vineyards,' where he looked for nothing but a small cell. But a divine revelation compelled him to return to the said town. Much as he liked the quiet of his little cell, he obeyed the command of God. He built a monastery not far from the city, and there he began to train many in a holy way of life, teaching the souls of his listeners more by deeds than by words. (7) He often withdrew, however, to a secret abode, which the neighbors called Burgum, a mile away from Favianis, in order to escape the people who came in such numbers to see him, and to draw nearer to God by uninterrupted prayer. Yet, lover of solitude that he was, he was often urged by revelations not to deny his presence to the people in their afflictions. (8) Thus his merit grew from day to day, and, likewise, the fame of his miracles—a fame that spread far and wide the news of divine grace manifested in his person. For what is good cannot remain unknown, as, according to the word of our Savior, a candle cannot be concealed under the measure, nor can a city set on a mountain be hidden.[6] (9) Among other great things that were granted him by the Savior was an extraordinary gift of abstinence. He subdued his flesh by innumerable fasts; he also taught that a body too richly fed was soon to bring the soul to ruin. (10) He never wore shoes

---

6 Matt. 5.14, 15.

at all; even in the middle of winter, which in those countries brings ice and severe frosts, he would always walk barefoot, and thus gave an impressive proof of endurance. The bitterness of that cold weather has a witness in the Danube, which often freezes with ice so deeply that it provides a safe crossing even for carts. (11) And yet he himself, raised to such excellence by the grace of God, acknowledged it with the greatest humility, saying: 'Do not think that what you see is in any way my own merit. It is rather an example for your salvation. Let the boldness of man give way, let the brow of pride be beaten. If we are capable of anything that is good, it is because we are chosen, as the Apostle says: "He has chosen us before the foundation of the world that we should be holy and without blemish in His sight."[7] Rather pray for me that my Savior's gifts may not add to my condemnation, but contribute to my justification.' (12) These and similar words he used to utter with tears and, in doing so, he taught the people a wonderful lesson in humility. Firmly secured in the foundation of this virtue, the splendor of his divine gift was so bright that even the enemies of the Church, the heretics, paid him the honor of their greatest respect.

5 (1) The king of the Rugi, Flaccitheus, felt unsafe in his power at the very beginning of his reign because the Goths from Lower Pannonia were violently hostile to him, and he was alarmed by their huge numbers. In this dangerous situation, he consulted the blessed Severin as a divine oracle. Once, being pressed very hard, the king came to him and told him with tears that he had requested from the leaders of the Goths to let him pass through their lands to Italy, and that, as his request had been denied, he had no doubt but that he was going to be killed. (2) To this he heard from the man of God the following reply: 'If we were united in the same Catholic faith, you ought to have consulted me rather about life in the next world; but since you are concerned only about this present life, which we both have in common, listen to what I

---

7 Eph. 1.4.

have to tell you. You will not be in danger from the Goths either because of their numbers or because of their hostility. They will soon depart, and you will rule safely in that prosperity for which you are wishing. But do not neglect the counsels of my humility. Do not think it beneath you to seek peace even with the weakest; never trust in your own strength. "Cursed," says Scripture, "be the man that trusteth in man, and maketh flesh his arm, and whose heart departeth from the Lord." Learn, therefore, to avoid traps, not to lay them; and you will find a peaceful end in your bed.' (3) The king went away with joy, much comforted by this prophecy, when he received news that a band of marauding barbarians had taken captive some of the Rugi. He at once sent to the man of God for advice. Severin, enlightened by the Lord, in a holy message warned him not to pursue the brigands, saying: 'If you pursue them, you will be killed. Beware: do not cross the river, and do not, for lack of caution, fall into the ambushes which have been prepared for you in three places. Soon a faithful messenger will come and inform you about all this.' (4) Then two prisoners who had escaped from the settlement of the enemies related in due order everything that the blessed man, informed by Christ, had foretold him. So the ambush of his opponents had come to nothing, and Flaccitheus, ever more prospering, finished his days in perfect peace.

6 (1) After this, there was a Rugian who had been tormented for twelve years by incredible pains of his bones and had been deprived of the use of all his limbs. During the long time that his intolerable torments lasted, they had become well known to his neighbors on all sides. Since various treatments had helped nothing, at last his widowed mother put her son in a cart, took him to the holy man, laid the incurable wretch down at the door of the monastery, and, crying all the time, she prayed that her only son be restored to her in good health. (2) The man of God, however, feeling that something great was asked of him, yet moved by her tears, said: 'Why do you

press me because of a fanciful notion that you have about me? Why am I supposed to be capable of something that I cannot do? It is not in my power to do such great things. I will, however, give you advice as one having obtained mercy from God.'[8] Then he tells the woman to make some gift to the poor according to her means. Without delay, she began to take off the clothing which she was wearing and quickly divided it among the needy. (3) When the man of God heard this, he was struck by her zeal; again he commanded her to cover herself with her clothes, and said: 'When your son, healed by the Lord, has gone on his way with you, then you will carry out the work that you have vowed.' He then announced a few days fast as he used to do, prayed fervently to God, and without delay healed the sick man, and as a healthy person, able to walk on his legs, he was sent home. (4) Often afterwards, when he went to the market, he gave proof of this incomprehensible miracle to all who saw him. Some would say: 'Look here, this is the fellow whose whole body was rotten.' Others would deny altogether that it was he, and there would arise a pleasant dispute. (5) From the time, then, that this man, who had been given up, was restored to health, the whole people of the Rugians began to visit frequently the servant of God in order to pay him their respect and to ask for his help when they were sick. Many of other races, too, whom the news of this great miracle had reached, wished to see the soldier of Christ.

(6)[9] Even before this had happened, some barbarians on their way to Italy, prompted by a similar reverence, turned aside in order to see him and to obtain his blessing. 7 (1) Among these there had come to him Odovacar, who afterwards ruled over Italy; but at that time he was a young man, of tall figure, clad in poor clothes. He stooped for fear to hit his head against the low roof of the humble cell. He was in-

---
8 Cf. 1 Cor. 7.25 (*a Domino*; but some manuscripts read *a Deo*).
9 This ought to be the opening paragraph of ch. 7, cf. Sauppe's edition and Baldermann, p. 152, n. 43.

formed by the holy man that he would become famous. When he took his leave, Severin again said to him: 'Go to Italy, go, now covered with mean hides; soon you will make rich gifts to many.'[10]

8 (1) King Feletheus, too, who was also called Feva, son of the said Flaccitheus, at the beginning of his reign imitated his father's regard for the holy man by paying him frequent visits. But he had a wicked and sinister queen, named Giso, who always held him back from salutary works of mercy. Among other stains of her wickedness, she had in mind to rebaptize (as heretics) some Catholics; but as her husband, out of reverence for Severin, did not give his consent, she quickly gave up her sacrilegious intention. (2) But she imposed hard conditions on the Romans; some of them she even ordered to be transported across the Danube. One day when she had come to a village near Favianis and had given orders to send some people to her across the Danube—for the purpose, to be sure, of being condemned to the lowest services of slavery—the man of God sent to her and asked her to let them go. She, however, burning with the fire of female fury, sent the messenger back with a harsh message: 'Pray for yourself,' she said, 'servant of God, hiding in your cell; let us dispose of our servants as we please.' (3) When the man of God heard this, he said: 'I trust in the Lord Jesus Christ that she will be compelled by necessity to fulfill what she has disdained in the vanity of her pride.' And swiftly came the punishment which struck down the arrogance of her mind. There were some goldsmiths of barbarian race whom she had put into strict custody for making royal jewels. Now on the same day that the queen had despised the servant of God, the little son of the said king, Fredericus, in childish curiosity entered their dungeon. The goldsmiths put a sword at the child's breast and said that if anybody dared to come in to them unless under

---

10 The German war leaders were expected to bestow gifts on their retainers; generosity was one of the virtues which a king was supposed to have.

the protection of an oath, they would first pierce the little prince and then kill themselves. This they would do because they saw no hope of survival for themselves, growing thinner everyday by their hard labor. (4) Hearing this, the cruel and godless queen tore her clothes with grief and cried out: 'O servant of the Lord, Severin, so does your God avenge an insult which He has suffered! This punishment, this of all, for my contempt you have demanded by instant prayers, to take vengeance in my offspring.' And running up and down in great remorse and with pitiful laments, she admitted that the punishment of the present disaster had come over her for the crime which she had committed in despising the servant of God. At once, she sent men on horseback to ask his pardon, sent back the Romans she had seized that same day—those for whom he had intervened and she had despised him—and then the goldsmiths received a promise under oath, let the child go free, and were themselves allowed to go.[11] (5) When the reverent servant of Christ heard this, he thanked his Creator profusely, who sometimes delays the fulfillment of a prayer in order that, after an increase of faith, hope, and charity, he may grant greater things where smaller things have been asked for. Thus the Savior in His omnipotence brought it about that the hard woman, who wanted to subject free persons to slavery, was forced to give servants of hers their freedom. (6) When these things had been miraculously achieved, the queen at once with her husband hurried to the servant of God,

---

11 The incident related in paragraphs 3 and 4 of this chapter resembles an episode in the German saga of Wieland (Veland) the smith. The hero, a craftsman of miraculous skill, becomes prisoner of a king, who maims him in order to prevent his escape, and has him work for his royal household. In revenge, Wieland lures the king's young sons to his abode, kills them, and then escapes on wings which he has secretly made. Cf. J. Grimm, *Deutsche Mythologie* (4. ed., Berlin 1875-78), 312-314; 399; W. Grimm, *Die deutsche Heldensage* (3. ed., Gütersloh 1889), 389; A. Heusler in J. Hoops, *Reallexikon der germanischen Altertumskunde* 4 (1919) 528ff.; E. H. Meyer, *Germanische Mythologie* (1903) 160ff. The parallel was first noted by Sommerlad, p. 19. Real connection, however, remains a mere possibility. (For literature on the Wieland saga, we are indebted to Professor Carl Selmer of Hunter College, New York.)

showed him her son, who, as she confessed, by his prayers had been rescued from the threshold of death, and promised never again to go against his commands.

9 (1) The servant of God, possessing a great gift of prophecy, showed also much concern in the liberation of captives. He strove eagerly to restore those suffering under servitude to barbarians to the freedom in which they had been born. In the course of such work, he gave orders to a man, whom with his wife and children he had ransomed, to cross[12] the Danube and to look in the market of the barbarians for an unknown person, whom, by divine revelation, he was able to describe so accurately that he could tell even details of his physique, the color of his hair, his features, the clothes he was wearing, and in what part of the market place he would find him. He added that the man should return to him at once and report what that person, having been found, would tell him. (2) So the man went and, to his surprise, found everything as the man of God had foretold him. As soon as he so surprisingly had found that man, he heard himself being addressed by him and asked: 'Do you think I can find somebody who, for any sum of money he might name, would lead me to the man of God whose fame is spreading everywhere? It is a long time that I am instantly beseeching these holy martyrs here, whose relics I carry with me, to be at last released from this service

---

12 *Transvadare*, the verb used by Eugippius here, need not necessarily mean 'to wade through,' but might be used with the wider meaning 'to cross.' Thus Victor Vitensis (*Historia persecutionis Africanae provinciae*, 1.1) says of the *Vandalica gens* that it landed in Africa *transvadans . . . per angustias maris* (the straits of Gibraltar). The verb is used several times in Euagrius' translation of Athanasius, *Vita s. Antonii* (12; 15; 60), where the verbs of the Greek original do not specify the mode of crossing; cf. also Pseudo-Ambrose, *De moribus Brachmanorum*, PL 17.1135A. St. Jerome's metaphor *diversos marina discrimina transvadantes inveniunt casus* (prologue to his revision of Victorinus of Pettau, *In Apocalypsin*, p. 14. 1 Haussleiter) is, likewise, based on this wider meaning. Similarly, Eugippius uses *transmeare* of the crossing of the Danube in a boat (*scafa*), 23.1. There is thus no need for postulating, with KW 1.123; 206f.; 2.132ff.; etc., a ford of the Danube near Favianis. (Much of the material for this note has kindly been supplied by the editor-in-general of the *Thesaurus Linguae Latinae*, Dr. W. Ehlers.)

of which I am unworthy, and which, so far, I have undertaken, not in bold presumption, but by a pious compulsion.' (3) Then the messenger of the man of God made himself known to him. St. Severin received with due honor the relics of the holy martyrs, Gervasius and Protasius, and placed them at the disposal of the priests in the basilica which he had built in his monastery. In that place, he united the shrines of many martyrs; he was always deigned to know about them beforehand by revelation; for he knew that the enemy often creeps in under the name of holiness. (4) He was also urged to accept the honorable office of bishop, but he settled the matter with a determined reply, saying that it was sufficient for him to have deprived himself of his beloved solitude and, by a divine call, to have come to this province in order to help the crowds of people who would turn to him in their tribulations. His monks, however, whom he wished to give a pattern of life, he admonished earnestly to take to the footsteps of the blessed fathers from whom one might acquire instruction in holy ways, and to be on their guard lest one who had left behind his parents and the world, looking back on the temptations of worldly pomp, might wish for the things he had decided to avoid; and as a deterring example, he put before them the wife of Lot.[13] (5) He also impressed on them the necessity of mortifying the impulses of passion for fear of the Lord, and maintained that the fires of sensual pleasure could be overcome only if by the grace of God they were quenched in a fountain of tears.

10 (1) There was a man named Maurus, janitor of the basilica of the monastery, whom blessed Severin had ransomed from the hands of the barbarians. To him one day the man of God gave the following instruction: 'Beware not to go out anywhere today; otherwise, you will not escape an imminent danger.' He, against the precept of such a good father, let himself be persuaded by a secular person to go out about mid-

---

[13] Cf. Athanasius, *Vita s. Antonii* 20 (Gen. 19.26; Luke 17.32).

day to pick fruit; they had gone only two miles from Favianis when suddenly he and the man who had persuaded him to go were captured by barbarians and carried off across the Danube. (2) At that hour, the man of God, reading in his cell, suddenly closed the book and said: 'Call Maurus to come to me quickly.' When the latter was found nowhere, he himself in great haste set across the Danube[14] and pursued the robbers, whom the people used to call 'Scamarae.' His venerable presence they could not bear, and humbly returned the prisoners they had taken.

11 (1) While the upper towns of Noricum Ripense were still standing, and hardly any fort escaped the attacks of the barbarians, the reputation of St. Severin had spread so far and wide that the single forts rivaled with each other to invite him for their protection; for they believed that in his presence no evil would befall them. This did not happen without the gracious will of God, because, as a consequence, all were awed by his commands as by heavenly oracles, and, following his example, they armed themselves with good works. (2) Among other places, the holy man had come to a fort called Cucullis, invited by the pious request of the people in its vicinity. There he worked a great miracle which I cannot leave untold. We have heard the amazing account from Marcianus, a citizen of that place, afterwards our priest. Some of the populace still adhered to the practice of abominable sacrifices in a certain place. When the man of God heard of this sacrilege, he frequently addressed the people, prevailed upon the priests of the locality to announce a three days' fast, and ordered every household to offer a candle, which each one with his own hand fixed on the walls of the church. (3) Then, as usual, the psalter was recited, and when

---

14 *Histri fluenta praetermeans.* Only here Eugippius uses for the Danube the name Hister. The Celtic *Danuvius* denoted the upper and middle course of the river, the Thracian *Hister* its lower course—corresponding to the habitats of the two peoples. Is Eugippius' phrase a literary reminiscence? Note that *praetermeans* does not fit in the context; Severin does not go along the river, he crosses it.

the hour of the sacrifice had come, the man of God invited the priests and deacons to pray with him to their common Lord with all the vigor of their hearts to show them the light of His knowledge so that they might know the lawless. When they, on their knees, had said long prayers with many tears, the greater number of the candles which the faithful had brought were suddenly kindled by the will of God; the remainder, however, those of the people stained by sacrilegious practices, who, anxious to remain unknown, had denied it, were left unkindled. (4) Those then, who had offered them, made known by the divine test, immediately cried out and, by their attempts to excuse themselves, gave away the secrets of their hearts; and being convicted by the testimony of their candles, they made an open confession and bore witness to their sacrilegious acts. (5) O clement power of the Creator, who kindles tapers as well as minds! A light was kindled in the tapers and shone to the senses. The visible light melted the wax to flames, but the invisible light dissolved into tears the hearts of those who confessed. Believe it or not,[15] those whom the error of sacrilege had held in bonds were afterwards more distinguished in good works than those whose candles had been divinely lighted.

12 (1) At some other time, locusts had settled in large numbers on the territory of the said fort; they consumed the crops and with their noxious bite laid everything waste. Struck by this pest, the priests and other inhabitants at once turned to St. Severin with urgent entreaties, saying: 'In order that this horrible plague may be removed from us, we ask the intercession of your prayers of which we have had proof; for we have seen in the miracle of the heavenly lighted tapers that your prayers count for much before the Lord.' (2) He addressed them piously: 'Have you not read,' he said, 'what divine authority has prescribed to a sinful people through

---

15 *Quis credat?* Mommsen's explanation (*Constat—quis credat?*—etc.) still holds good. The insertion of a negative particle (*Quis non credat* . . . Schuster) misses the point.

the Prophet: "Be converted to me with all your heart, in fasting and in weeping," and a little later: "Sanctify a fast, He saith, call an assembly, gather the congregation,"[16] and all that follows? Therefore, fulfill with worthy actions what you teach that you may perhaps escape the evil of the present time. And let nobody, on any account, go out on his field as if he could ward off the locusts by human effort, lest God's wrath be provoked even more.' (3) Without delay everybody gathered in the church, and they all, each in his place, recited the psalms as was the custom. Every age and sex, even those who could not yet speak, offered a prayer to God with tears, alms were given unceasingly, and every good work which the present emergency demanded was carried out as had been prescribed by the servant of God. (4) Whereas all were engaged in efforts of this kind, one very poor man left the work of God half done and went out to his field to look after his crop, a tiny parcel of land between the fields of the others. The whole day he spent anxiously chasing away as best he could the cloud of locusts that hung over them; then he went back to church for communion. But his little crop, amidst the crops of the neighbors, was eaten by a swarm of locusts. In that night, the locusts were removed from that district by divine command—which proves the great power of faithful prayer. (5) In the morning, when the violator and scorner of the holy work with misgivings went out to his field again, he found it totally destroyed by the pernicious locusts, and the crops of the others all around he found intact. Greatly astonished, he returned to the fort with mournful lament, and when he had reported what had happened, all went out to see such a miracle: the locusts had marked with their bites, as if with a straight rod, the crop of the scorner. (6) Then, going down on his knees before them all, he begged, with laments, their intercession in order that his sin might be forgiven. Therefore, the man of God took his opportunity of

---

16 Joel 2.12, 15.

an admonition and taught them all that they should learn to obey Almighty God, whose orders were obeyed even by locusts. The said pauper, however, pleaded his case: how could he obey God's commandments in the future if no hope of livelihood was left for him? (7) Then the man of God said to the others: 'It is only fair that he who by his punishment has given you an example of humility and obedience should receive this year's livelihood by your liberality.' A collection was made among the faithful, and the poor man, chastised as well as enriched by it, learnt what damage incredulity might bring, and what benefits the bounty of God might bestow upon His worshipers.

13[17] (1) Near a town called Iuvao, one day they went to church in summer for the evening service and could not find fire for lighting the lamps. Neither did they succeed in striking fire out of stones, and in striking them [iron and stone] together,[18] they delayed so much that the time of the solemn evening service elapsed. (2) The man of God, however, kneeling on the floor, prayed intently. Suddenly, in the presence of three spiritual men who happened to be there at the time, the taper which St. Severin held in his hand was lighted. By its light, the evening sacrifice was performed according to custom, and thanks were rendered to God for everything. Although he wanted those who had witnessed the miracle to keep it secret (as he did in the case of many another great work which God's power gloriously worked through him), yet the splendor of such a miracle could not be hidden, but kindled others mightily to great faith.

---

17 A close parallel to this miracle is found in the Life of St. Alveus (Gaul, sixth century): AS Sept. 3. 808.
18 The words *ferri* (*om.* II) *ac petrae* (used here alone with the Romance meaning of *pierre* 'flint') have been recognized as a gloss by Vetter. They certainly contradict the statement immediately preceding. I do not think, however, as does Noll, that a reference to steel is excluded by the ritual character of the act. The context makes it quite clear that the clerics had expected to find fire and acted in an emergency. Neither do I agree with Noll's interpretation of *alterutra . . . conlisione* 'by their mutual jostling.'

14 (1) It also happened that a woman of the same locality, who had suffered from a long sickness, lay half-dead, and the funeral was already prepared. Her relatives, in mournful silence, buried funeral laments under the voice of faith, and placed the body that was almost exhausted by the illness at the doorstep of the saintly man's monastery. (2) The man of God, seeing the entrance blocked by the bed, said to them: 'What is it that you have decided to do?' They answered: 'That by your prayers the dead should be given back to life.' Then he said with tears: 'Why do you demand a great thing of a lowly man? I know I am utterly unworthy. If I could only find pardon for my sins.' And they: 'We believe,' they said, 'that she will revive if you pray.' (3) Then St. Severin at once threw himself down on the ground in prayer, with tears, and the woman immediately arose. He addressed her thus: 'Do not attribute any of these things to my own doing. It is the fervor of your faith that has deserved this grace, and this has happened in many places and among many races in order that it may be made known that there is one God, who works miracles in heaven and on earth, who raises the damned to salvation and restores the dead to life.' The woman, however, who had recovered her health, after three days resumed work in the fields with her own hands as was the custom of the province.

15 (1) Quintanis was the name of a municipality in Raetia Secunda, on the bank of the Danube; near it was the course of a small river named Businca. This river often swelled when the Danube went high and overflowed, and would then cover some parts of the fort which was built in the plain. The inhabitants of that place also had constructed a church of wood outside the walls which, in its whole extension, was a suspended structure. It was supported by posts driven into the ground which branched out into forks; over this structure, there was a sort of floor—planed boards joined together. Whenever the river overflowed, this floor was covered by the floods. (2) The faithful people of Quintanis had invited St.

Severin to their place. He came at a time of dry weather, and asked why the floor was left without a cover. The people of the neighborhood answered that, by the frequent inundation of the river, any cover they might put on was always washed away by the flood. He, however, said: 'Have a pavement laid now over the boards in Christ's name. You will see that from now on the river is kept off by a divine command.' (3) When the pavement was finished, he himself descended underneath the aisle, took an axe in his hand, said a prayer, struck the posts, cut into the wood the sign of the venerable cross, and said to the water of the river: 'My Lord Jesus Christ does not allow thee to rise above this sign of the cross.' (4) From that time, whenever the river rose high as before and flooded the vicinity as it used to, it was so much lower than the level of the church that it never overpassed the sign of the cross which the man of God had marked.

16 (1) It so happened that the priest of that fort, a very venerable man named Silvinus, came to die. When he was laid out on his bier in the church and they had kept the vigil with psalm-singing as was the custom, at daybreak the man of God asked the tired priests and deacons to retire for a little while and to have some sleep for their relaxation after the hardship of the vigil. (2) When they had gone, the man of God asked the *ostiarius,* named Maternus, whether all had gone as he had told them. The latter answered that all had gone away, but St. Severin said: 'Not so. A woman is hiding here.' Then the doorkeeper made another round of the precincts of the church and assured him that nobody had remained within. But the soldier of Christ, informed by a revelation of the Lord, said: 'Somebody is hiding here.' So the doorkeeper searched a third time with even greater diligence and found a consecrated virgin hiding in one of the less conspicuous places. (3) The doorkeeper reproached her: 'What are you doing? Did you expect that your presence would remain secret when the servant of God was here?' She said: 'It was love of religion that caused me to do this. For when I saw that all were sent outside, I thought by myself that the servant of God would invoke God's majesty to raise this dead man here to life.' (4) So, when the said virgin had also gone, the man of God, together with the priest and the deacon and the two doorkeepers, bent down and prayed with a flood of tears that the power from above might give the often-proved manifestation of its majesty. Then, as the priest was ending his prayer, the blessed man addressed the dead body with these words: 'In the name of our Lord Jesus Christ, holy priest Silvinus, speak to your brethren.' (5) The dead man opened his eyes; the man of God was hardly able to persuade those present to keep silent, so great was their joy. Again, Severin said to the dead man: 'Do you want us to ask the Lord to grant you again to His servants in this life?' He, however, said: 'I adjure you by the Lord, do not let me be kept here any longer, and be cheated of eternal rest in which I already saw myself placed.' (6) He had hardly said these words when he lay again without life. This event was kept secret by the express will of St. Severin, who forebade to make it known before his death. I heard the story as I have told it from the accounts of the subdeacon, Marcus, and the janitor, Maternus. For the priest and the deacon, who had been witnesses of this great miracle, died, as is known, before the holy man who had their promise not to reveal to anybody what they had seen.

17 (1) Blessed Severin, on whom such wonderful gifts had been bestowed generously by the grace of Christ, had also, in his inborn goodness, taken upon himself the care of the captives and the needy—so much so that, throughout the towns and forts, almost all the poor were supported by his personal efforts. He served them with such cheerful concern that he never thought himself saturated [or wealthy in good things][19] until he saw the bodily needs of all the poor provided for. (2) Whereas he himself was not broken by fasting for a whole

---
19 The words within brackets have been recognized as a gloss by von Winterfeld, cf. the apparatus in Noll[2] *ad loc.*

week in succession, he thought himself afflicted by the hunger of those in misery. Most people, seeing his pious generosity towards the needy, though themselves suffering from lack of food under the harsh rule of the barbarians, would as yet religiously give one tenth of their corn to the poor. This precept, though well known to all from the Law, was observed with greater zeal when they heard it from the mouth, as it were, of an angel who had come to them. (3) The man of God also felt the cold only in the nakedness of the poor, having received the special grace from God to keep strong and alive in a very cold climate—a wonderful proof of mortification. (4) For the collection of the tithes, as has been said, by which the poor were supported, he used to urge even the people of Noricum (Mediterraneum) by letters. This had become a custom. One day, when they had sent him a number of clothes for distribution, he asked those who had come whether a similar collection was being sent also from the town of Tiburnia. They answered that men from that place ought to be there any moment; but the man of God pointed out to them that they would not come, but that their belated offering would have to be handed over to the barbarians. Soon afterwards, the citizens of Tiburnia, after an undecided fight with the Goths by whom they had been besieged, just barely managed to conclude a peace treaty, under the terms of which, among other things, they were obliged to hand over to the enemy the alms which they had already collected, but which they had delayed to send to the servant of God.

18 (1) The inhabitants of the town of Lauriacum, in spite of frequent reminders from St. Severin, had delayed the offering to the poor of their tithes of corn. They were plagued with famine, but, as the ripening crops were already turning yellow, relief seemed near. Now when the pest of rust suddenly appeared on the corn and threatened to destroy it, they at once went to him, threw themselves at his feet, and confessed that this was the punishment for their contempt. (2) The soldier of Christ comforted the weary ones with spiritual

words, saying: 'If you had offered your tithes to the poor, you would not only reap eternal reward, but also enjoy temporal goods in plenty. But as you have denounced your sin by your own confession, I promise, from the goodness of our Lord, that the fierce rust will do no damage this time; only, let your faith not waver in the future.' This promise made the citizens all the more readily disposed to pay their tithes from that day on. Then, as he used to do, he urged them to announce a fast; when this was over, a soft rain destroyed the pest of the crops which had already been given up.

19 (1) Batavis is the name of a town situated between the two rivers, Inn and Danube. There blessed Severin had built a monastery for a few monks in his usual manner because he was often asked by the citizens to come to that place, especially in view of the frequent invasions of the Alamanni, whose king, Gibuldus, greatly honored and loved him. (2) At one time the king, wishing ardently to see Severin, even went there to see him. The saint, fearing that the king's coming might be a burden to the city, went outside to meet him. He addressed the king so firmly that the latter began to tremble vehemently in his presence; after they had parted, the king declared to his army that never before, either in battle or in any peril, had he been shaken by such trembling. (3) When he gave the servant of God his choice to demand of him what he wanted, the wise teacher asked him that, in his own interest, he should restrain his people from the devastation of Roman territory, and that he should graciously release those who were being held prisoners by his men. Then the king decided that Severin should send one of his own companions in order to carry out this plan as soon as possible. Without delay, the deacon, Amantius, was dispatched, who followed in the king's path; but he had to sit at his door for many days, and did not succeed in getting admission. (4) When he most sadly returned because he had not achieved the thing for which he had been sent, a person appeared to him who looked exactly like St. Severin; he frightened him with threats and bade him

follow. As he followed in fear and excitement, he came to the king's door, and there the guide who had led him the way suddenly, to his surprise, disappeared from his sight. The king's messenger asked the deacon where he came from and what was his desire. He briefly explained his business, handed in his letters, received the king's[20] letters in turn, and went home. (5) He came back with about seventy prisoners, and also with a welcome promise from the king to the effect that he would have the province searched carefully, and would then return all and every prisoner that he might find there. In that affair the holy priest, Lucillus, was dispatched afterwards; he recovered a great number of unfortunate people from captivity.

20 (1) At the time when the Roman Empire was still in existence, the soldiers of many towns were supported by public money for their watch along the wall. When this arrangement ceased, the military formations were dissolved and, at the same time, the wall was allowed to break down. The garrison of Batavis, however, still held out. Some of these had gone to Italy to fetch for their comrades the last payment, but on their way they had been routed by the barbarians, and nobody knew. (2) One day when St. Severin was reading in his cell, he suddenly closed the book and began to sigh heavily and to shed tears. He told those who were present to go speedily to the river,[21] which, as he declared, was at that hour red with human blood. And at that moment, the news arrived that the bodies of the said soldiers had been washed ashore by the current of the river.

21 (1) Paulinus, a priest, had come to St. Severin, attracted by his spreading fame. Having stayed some days in the company of the blessed man, and wishing to go home, he was told by him: 'Hurry, venerable priest, for soon, my beloved friend, will you be adorned by the dignity of episcopal rank,

---

20 *regis* (*regi* Mommsen with some manuscripts) is regarded as a (misplaced) gloss by Vetter: Noll2, p. 29.
21 The Inn, not the Danube.

much as the will of the people—so we believe—may be against your wish.' (2) Paulinus had hardly come home when the words of the prophet concerning him were fulfilled. For the citizens of Tiburnia, which is the metropole of Noricum, forced the said man to accept the eminency of being their high priest.

22 (1) For the basilica outside the walls of Batavis, in a place called Boiotro, across the river Inn, where he had built a small abode for a few monks, relics of martyrs were sought. Priests volunteered to be sent in search of holy relics; but blessed Severin uttered these words of warning: 'Although everything built by the hands of mortals will pass away, these buildings will have to be abandoned more quickly than others'; and, therefore, he said, they should not take any trouble in procuring the relics of saints, because the blessed relics of St. John would come to them by themselves. (2) Meanwhile, the inhabitants of that town humbly approached the blessed man to go to Feba, prince of the Rugi, and demand for them a permission for trade. He said to them: 'The time has come near when this town will lie abandoned like all the upper forts which have been deserted by their inhabitants. What point is there in providing merchandise for places where no merchant will be able to make an appearance in future?' (3) They answered that they ought not to be slighted, but be supported by his guidance as before; and a priest, filled with the spirit of the devil, added: 'Go, saint, I beg, go quickly that by your departure we may get a little rest from fasts and vigils.' At these words, the man of God was moved to floods of tears because a priest had given vent to his ridiculous vanity before a whole audience. For open scurrility bears witness to hidden sins. When, therefore, the holy man was asked by his brethren why he thus cried, he said: 'I see a great disaster come over this place as soon as we shall have left, and the sanctuaries of Christ—to my grief I am compelled to say so—will be flooded with human blood; even this place will be violated.' For he was speaking in the baptistery. (4) He sailed down the Danube to his oldest and biggest monastery, outside the walls of the town of Favianis, which was a hundred miles and more away.[22] Soon afterwards, when he was still sailing down the river, Hunumundus with a few barbarians in his company, invaded the town of Batavis, as the saint had foretold them; since almost all the inhabitants were out at the harvest, the forty men who had remained as guard of the town were killed. (5) The priest who had spoken such blasphemous words against the servant of Christ in the baptistery took refuge to that very same place; but the barbarians pursued him and killed him there. In vain did the enemy of truth, who had offended God, take refuge in the place which he had left so shamelessly.

23 (1) One day St. Severin, reading the Gospel in his monastery at Favianis, after offering prayer arose and ordered a boat to be made ready for him; when they wondered he said: 'Blessed be the name of the Lord:[23] we must go to meet the relics of the blessed martyrs.' They crossed the Danube without delay and found a man sitting on the opposite bank of the river who asked them, with many entreaties, to be led to the servant of God, to whom, on account of his fame with all people, he had long wished to come. (2) The servant of Christ was pointed out to him, and he humbly offered him relics of St. John Baptist, which he had kept with him for a long time. The servant of God received them with due reverence, and solemnly dedicated to the service of the priests the basilica of St. John,[24] whose blessed relics, as he had prophesied, had come without their asking.

24 (1) Warned by one of his revelations, the man of God also sent to the people of a town called Ioviaco, twenty miles or more from Batavis, a man named Moderatus, chanter of the church, with the message that they all should without de-

---

22 In fact, ca. 150 miles.
23 Ps. 112.2.
24 Since Severin was no bishop, he could not have performed the liturgical consecration of the basilica. *Sacrare* here is not to be understood in this technical meaning. Thus far, Winter (KW 2.289-291) is right.

lay abandon that place; if they despised his order, they would soon perish. (2) When some of them doubted this great prophecy, others openly disbelieved, he again sent a man of Quintanis, to whom he said with tears: 'Go quickly and give them this message: If they stay there overnight, they will without delay be taken captive.' He also gave orders to urge instantly holy Maximianus, a priest of spiritual life, that he at least should part company with the scorners and hasten to be rescued by the mercy of heaven; the man of God let him know that on this point he felt a great sadness, fearing he might put off his salutary command and fall a victim to the impending catastrophe. (3) The said man went, carried out his orders, and when the others still could not bring themselves to believing him and the priest tried to keep back the messenger of the man of God and offered him his hospitality, he firmly resisted the offer. In that night, the Heruli made an unexpected attack, laid the town waste, took most of the people prisoners, and hanged the said priest on a cross. When the servant of God heard this, he was very much grieved that they had not minded his warnings.

25 (1) Then a man from Noricum named Maximus, who used to visit the servant of God, once came to him, and being a close friend of his, and deservedly so, stayed several days in the monastery of the holy man. There he was informed by Severin that his country was soon to experience a grave disaster. He received a letter for the holy bishop, Paulinus, and returned speedily. (2) The said bishop, instructed by this letter, wrote in his own name to all the forts of his whole diocese and urged them earnestly, as had been indicated in the letter of the man of God, to avert the approaching disaster by a three days' fast. (3) They obeyed his orders, and when the fast had been completed, lo, a huge host of Alamanni laid sadly waste the whole country, but the forts, confidently protected against the fierce enemy by the armor of pious fasting and commendable humility of heart as they had been advised by the prophetic man, escaped all peril.

473?

26 (1) After this, a leper from the territory of Milan, attracted by the fame of St. Severin, traveled to him, and humbly implored him to restore his health. Severin ordered a fast and commended him to his monks. At once, by the grace of God, he was cleansed. When, being healed, he was told to return home, he threw himself at the holy man's feet and asked not to be forced to go back to his former life, wishing to be freed of the leprosy of sin as he had been freed of the leprosy of his body, and to end his life laudably in the place where he was. (2) The man of God greatly admired his religious spirit, and with fatherly authority gave orders to a few monks to stay with him in continuous prayer and with frequent fasts in order that the Lord might grant the man what was good for him. Fortified by these great remedies, before the end of two months he was freed from the fetters of mortal life.

27 (1) At the same time, the inhabitants of the town of Quintanis, tired at last by the frequent invasions of the Alamanni, left their homes and moved to Batavis. But their place of refuge did not remain unknown to the barbarians; it was for them even a greater incitement, for they believed they could now plunder the people of two towns in one attack. Blessed Severin, however, praying more instantly than ever, fortified the Romans with his good example, and foretold them that the present enemies would be defeated with the help of God, but that, after the victory, those who despised his warnings would perish. (2) All the Romans, therefore, strengthened by the prophecy of the holy man and by the hope of the victory they had been promised, drew up in battle line against the Alamanni, protected not so much by material weapons as by the prayers of the holy man. In that battle, the Alamanni were defeated and turned to flight, and the man of God thus addressed the victors: 'My sons, do not attribute to your own strength your victory in this present battle, but know that you have been freed now by the help of God in order that within this short lapse of time, during a truce, as it were, which you have obtained, you may go away from here. Gather, therefore, around me and go with me down to the city of Lauriacum.' This warning, full of piety, was given by the man of God. But the people of Batavis were reluctant to abandon their native soil; he, therefore, added: 'Although even that town for which we now make will soon have to be abandoned before the growing tide of barbarism, let us go now all the same!' At this warning, most people followed him. Some, however, remained stubborn, and the sword of the enemy did not fail to punish them for their contempt. For all those who remained there against the warning of the man of God were punished for their scorn when the Thoringi made an attack during the very same week; some were killed, others were carried into captivity.

28 (1) After the destruction of the towns in the upper region of the Danube, St. Severin constantly warned all the people who, obeying his instructions, had migrated to the town of Lauriacum not to trust in their own power but, being intent on prayer, fasts, and almsgiving, to fortify themselves rather with spiritual weapons. (2) One day the man of God ordered all the poor to be assembled in a basilica in order to deal them out their ration of oil. This commodity[25] was hard to obtain in those places because merchants had great difficulty in importing it. Now, as if a blessing was to be gained, a big crowd of needy people had gathered; for the precious food that this liquor was had greatly increased the number of beggars. (3) When the holy man had finished the prayer and had made the sign of the cross, in the presence of all he uttered the words of Sacred Scripture: 'Blessed be the name of the Lord!'[26] Then he began to deal out the oil with his own hand to the ministers who carried it around, imitating, as a faithful servant, his Lord, who had come not to be served but to serve,[27] and, following in the footsteps of the Savior, he

---
25 *Species.* The word has come to mean 'spice' even in late antiquity, especially in legal texts.
26 Ps. 112.2.
27 Matt. 20.28; Mark 10.45.

saw to his joy that the substance which his right hand poured out without his left hand knowing[28] was increased. For whilst the vessels of the poor were filling, there was no less in the hands of his ministers. (4) Whereas all the bystanders silently admired this great gift of God, one of them, Pientissimus by name, overcome with great astonishment, called out: 'My Lord, this pot of oil increases and overflows like a fountain!' In this way, the welcome flow of the liquor stopped because the miracle had been made known. (5) At once, the servant of Christ exclaimed: 'What have you done, brother? You have prevented the advantage of many. May the Lord Jesus Christ forgive you.' In the same way, the widow burdened with debts was instructed by the prophet Eliseus[29] to fill with a drop of oil that she had left as many vessels as possible. When she had done this and asked her sons for more vessels, and was told that there were no more, the oil stood.[30]

29 (1) At the same time, Maximus of Noricum, whom we have mentioned above, kindled by the fire of his faith, traveled to blessed Severin in the middle of winter, when the roads of that country are closed by the numbing cold. He was prompted to do so by his daring rashness, or rather, as became evident later, by his unshakable faith. He took with him many companions who, on their backs, carried clothes for the benefit of the captives and the poor—the result of a pious collection among the Norici. When on their way they reached the heights of the Alps, so much snow had fallen there throughout the night that they, who had sheltered under a big tree, found themselves closed in by the snow as if they were in a huge pit. (2) They gave up all hope of survival as there was apparently no help; then the leader of the convoy saw in his sleep a man of the shape of the man of God standing before him and saying to him: 'Do not be afraid, continue the journey which you have begun.' Instantly relieved by this

---
28 Matt. 6.3.
29 i.e. Elisha.
30 4 Kings 4.2-7.

revelation, they resumed their march, traveling in the strength of their faith rather than with their feet. Suddenly, by divine command, the huge shape of a bear appeared by their side to show them the way—although this animal usually hides in caves during the winter. He at once opened up a way for them, and for about two hundred miles,[31] he did not stray either left or right, but led them the desired road. (3) He walked before them just at the right interval for preparing their way by his fresh footsteps. Thus the wild beast marched through the vast solitude and never deserted the men who were bringing relief to the needy, but led them on as intelligibly for men as he could until they came to human habitations; then, his duty done, he suddenly went afield. By fulfilling this service of guide, he gave an example of what men are obliged to do for their fellowmen, and what a debt of charity they owe each other, since a wild beast led the way to people in despair. (4) When their arrival was announced to the man of God, he said: 'Blessed be the name of the Lord![32] Let in those for whom a bear opened the way by which they might come.' Hearing this, they were greatly astonished at the reference made by the man of God to something that had happened in his absence.

30 (1) The people of the town of Lauriacum and of the upper forts used to send out scouts to places thought to be in danger, and in this way tried to take every precaution that was humanly possible against the enemy. The man of God, by the divine inspiration of his prophetic mind, instructed them to bring all their modest belongings within the walls so that the enemy on their deadly expedition, finding no means of human support, would at once be compelled by famine to give up their cruel plans. (2) Having urged this for four days, on the evening of the fourth day, he sent a monk called Valens to holy Constantius, the bishop of that place, and to

---
31 The figure is impossible; it possibly results from a scribal blunder, cf. Noll, p. 179f.
32 Ps. 112.2.

the others who were assembled with him: 'Tonight distribute guards along the walls and watch very carefully, then you will be safe from the onslaught of the enemy who is approaching.' They, however, strongly affirmed that their scouts had reported no indications of any danger. (3) But the servant of Christ did not cease to warn them against their indifference, and exclaimed with a loud voice, affirming that they would be caught that same night if they did not obey faithfully his commands, often repeating: 'Stone me,' he said, 'stone me if I am found to have lied.' So, at long last, they felt compelled to keep watch on the walls. The customary service of psalms at the beginning of the night was already over, and they had begun their watch in great numbers when a stack of hay nearby, lit accidentally by the torch of a porter, gave light to the town without starting a fire. (4) When, at this moment, all began to shout, the enemy, hidden under the trees of the forests, was frightened by the sudden light and noise. They thought they had been sighted and, therefore, kept quiet; and on the following morning, they swarmed around the city in all directions, and, finding no food, they took the cattle of one man who, in spite of the warning of the man of God, had boldly neglected to rescue his property, and then went away. When they were gone, the townspeople went out of the gates; not far from the walls, they found ladders lying on the ground which the barbarians had brought along when preparing to sack the town, and which they had thrown away during the night, terrified by the shouting of the guards. (5) The townspeople humbly asked pardon of the servant of Christ, and confessed that their hearts were harder than stone. By the present event, they had learnt that the gift of prophecy was strong in the holy man. The entire population, through their disobedience, would now all be prisoners had not, as always, the prayer of the man of God preserved their freedom; as the Apostle James declares: 'The unceasing prayer of a just man,' he says, 'is of great avail.'[33]

---

33 James 5.16.

31 (1) When Feletheus, king of the Rugi, also called Feva, heard that the remnants of the people of all the towns that had escaped the sword of the barbarians, on the advice of the servant of God, had gone to Lauriacum, he came with his army—with the idea of taking them by surprise and carrying them with him in order to place them in the cities that paid him tribute and were near to him; one of these was Favianis, separated from the Rugi by nothing but the Danube. (2) About this, all the people were greatly upset and humbly approached St. Severin to meet the king on his way and persuade him to make a less drastic decision. Severin hurried along the whole night and met the king twenty miles from the town in the early morning. The king got a shock when he saw him come, and confessed that he was much grieved about Severin's wearisome journey, and he asked him what was the cause of this unexpected meeting. (3) The servant of God said: 'Peace be to you, best of kings! I come as a messenger of Christ, begging mercy for those who are entrusted to me. Think of God's grace, call to your mind the divine favors by which your father often felt himself supported. For during all the years of his reign, he never dared do anything without consulting me. And as he did not resist my salutary warnings, he learnt the great value of obedience; he also learnt that a victor, for his own good, should not get proud by his victories.' (4) The king said: 'I shall not allow this people, for whom you have come as a loving advocate, to be robbed by the plundering Alamanni and Thoringi, or to be slain by the sword, or led into slavery. We have tributary towns in the vicinity where they are to be settled.' (5) The servant of Christ replied firmly: 'Have these people been rescued from the frequent raids of plunderers by your bow or sword? Have they not rather been preserved by the favor of God so that they may obey you for a short while? Well, then, best of kings, do not reject my advice. Give these subjects into my trust, lest they, being in the hands of such a big army, be routed rather than transplanted. I trust in my Lord that He, who made me come to their assistance in their distress, will make me an able guarantor for their being led to safety.' (6) To these modest representations, the king gave way, and immediately went back with his army. Consequently, the Romans whom St. Severin had taken in his trust left Lauriacum; they were distributed over the towns by a peaceful settlement[34] and lived on friendly terms with the Rugi. He himself stayed at Favianis, in his old monastery, and unceasingly admonished the people and foretold the future, declaring that they all would migrate to a province of the Roman land without loss of liberty.

after 476   32 (1) At that time, king Odovacar wrote a friendly letter to St. Severin, humbly offering him his choice of a petition if he thought he had one to make. He had not forgotten that prophecy by which Severin had once indicated that Odovacar would be king. Encouraged by this address, the saint asked him to pardon a certain Ambrosius and recall him from exile. Odovacar gladly obeyed his command. (2) Once, when many nobles, as is common, praised that king in flattering terms in the presence of the holy man, he asked what king it was whom they praised so exceedingly. They answered: 'Odovacar.' 'Odovacar,' he said, 'is safe between thirteen and fourteen,' meaning the years he was to reign undisturbed; and he added that they would soon see his prophecy fulfilled.

33 (1) The townspeople of Comagenis, where he had first been known, humbly asked blessed Severin to come, and he came. When his presence became known, one of the nobles of king Feletheus, whose young son was suffering from a long illness, and for whom he already prepared the funeral, took him across the Danube, placed him at Severin's feet, and said with tears: 'I believe, man of God, that you will obtain from God a quick recovery for my son.' (2) Severin prayed, and he who had been brought in half dead, to the great astonishment

---

34 *Benivola societate.* Winter (KW 2.434; 450 under *civilitas*) compares the peaceful coexistence of Goths and Romans in Theoderic's Italy.

of his father, rose up healed and returned home in perfect health.

34 (1) A leper named Teio came from afar, encouraged by the miracles of St. Severin, and asked to be cleansed by his prayers. So he was given the usual command, namely, to pray ceaselessly to God, the dispenser of all grace. (2) Why say more? By the prayers of the blessed man, the leper, with God's help, was cleansed, and as he changed his character for the better, he deserved to change also his color; and he proclaimed publicly with his own tongue, as did also many others, the great works of the eternal king.

35 (1) Bonosus, a monk of blessed Severin, by birth a barbarian, who hung upon his words, suffered gravely from bad eyesight and asked to be healed by his prayer. He felt sore seeing that strangers and outsiders experienced the aid of his healing grace whereas Severin would never come to his rescue and heal him. (2) The servant of God said to him: 'It is not good for you, my son, to have a clear sight in your bodily eyes and to see well externally. Rather pray that your inner eye may be strengthened.' Instructed by these and similar admonitions, he strove to see with his heart rather than with his eye, and he was miraculously rewarded by the gift of long continual prayer without tiring; and after serving steadfastly in the monastery for about forty years, he deceased with the same ardor of faith which he had when he entered.

36 (1) In Boiotro, a place mentioned above, the humble teacher found three monks of his monastery infected with horrible pride. He took them one by one and blamed them, but when he saw that they persisted in their state of death, he prayed that the Lord, receiving them among his adopted sons, should deign to bring them to reason with His paternal flail. Even before he had ended his tearful prayer, these monks were suddenly seized by an evil spirit and, tormented by him, made known by their words the stubbornness of their hearts. (2) Let nobody think it cruel or harmful that men of this kind were given 'to Satan for the destruction of the flesh,' as the blessed apostle teaches,[35] 'that the spirit may be saved in the day of our Lord Jesus.' Blessed Ambrose, bishop of Milan, said that a slave of Stilicho who had been found to have forged letters ought to be delivered unto Satan so that in future he may not dare to do this again; at that very moment, when the word had hardly come from the priest's[36] mouth, the unclean spirit seized him and began to torment him. (3) Also Severus Sulpicius relates,[37] from the account of Postumianus, that a man who had the wondrous gift of performing signs and miracles, wishing to expel from his heart the vanity of pride by which he had been seized, prayed that for five months he should be given into the power of the devil and become like those whom he himself had cured. A little further, the same author says: 'Seized by a spirit, put into chains, he suffered all the things which the possessed usually suffer; at last, after five months, he was cured, not only of the demon, but, what was more to his advantage and to his wish, of his pride.' (4) The man of God then gave these monks into the care of some brethren and for forty days subjected them to the bitter medicine of fast. At the end of that time, he prayed over them, freed them from the power of the evil spirit, and gave them health, not only of their bodies, but also of their minds. This incident increased the reverent awe in which the holy man was held, and the others were filled with a greater fear of discipline.

37 (1) The monk, Marcianus, who afterwards, as a priest, was head of the monastery before us, had been sent by him to Noricum together with brother Renatus. When the third day had passed, Severin said to the brethren: 'Pray, beloved ones, for a great tribulation has come over Marcianus and Renatus in this hour; but with the help of Christ they will be freed.' (2) The monks at once wrote down what he had

---

35 1 Cor. 5.5.
36 Paulinus, *Vita s. Ambrosii* 43. The deacon, Paulinus, was secretary to St. Ambrose.
37 *Dialogi* 1.20.7.

said, and when, after several months, the two returned, they confirmed the day and hour when they had a narrow escape from the barbarians.

38 (1) Blessed Severin once unexpectedly bade one of the brethren, Ursus by name, to prevent a threatening calamity by a strict fast with abstinence from food and with lamentations, saying: 'You are threatened by a peril for your body, which you can avert with the help of God by the remedy of scarce bread and water.' On the fortieth day, a deadly pustule appeared on the arm of the fasting brother, who at once went to Severin and humbly showed it to him. (2) The holy servant of God said to him: 'Do not be afraid of this peril which I announced to you forty days ago.' At once he made the sign of the cross over it with his hand, and to the astonishment of all present the deadly pustule disappeared. Be it sufficient to have told this one instance of a healing in his own house, in order to avoid the annoyance of an over-long book. For he often foresaw, by a revelation of Christ, illnesses of his monks, and by the same gift by which he foresaw them he also cured them.

39 (1) The spiritual teacher dwelled not far from the cells of his disciples, persevering over long periods in prayer and abstinence. Together with them, however, he performed the morning prayers and the appropriate psalms at the beginning of the night. The remaining times of prayer he observed in the little oratory where he lived. At those times he often, assured by heavenly oracles, foretold, by the grace of God, future events; he also knew the secrets of many, and, when necessary, brought them to light and provided remedies for everyone of them according as the nature of his disease would require. (2) He had only one single rug of rough hair on the pavement of his oratory. All the time he wore one and the same cloak, even when he was sleeping. Never, except on certain feast days, would he break his fast before sunset. During the periods of the forty days' fast, he was content with one meal a week, and yet his face shone with the same cheerfulness as at other times. He wept over the sins of others as if they were his own, and helped them to overcome their faults by every means he knew.

40 (1) When at last, after many contests and long fights, blessed Severin knew by God's revelation that he was about to leave this world, he summoned to him the said king of the Rugi, Feva, with his cruel wife, Giso. (2) Having made to the king some salutary exhortations, namely, that he should deal with his subjects in such a way as he would think fit for one who was to account for the state of his realm before the Lord, and having warned him without fear, he stretched out his hand, pointed at the king's breast, and asked his queen sternly: 'What do you love more, Giso: this heart, or gold and silver?' Now, as she said that she preferred her husband to any treasures, the man of God, in his wisdom, said: 'Then cease to oppress the innocent, for their affliction might break up your power. You often bring to nothing the clemency of the king.' (3) She, however, said: 'Why do you, man of God, give us this reception?' He replied: 'I beseech you in all humility, now that I am about to go to God, to refrain from acts of injustice and to be intent on pious works. So far, your realm has flourished by God's will: from this fact you ought to judge.' Well instructed by these warnings, the king and his queen bade him farewell and left. (4) After that, the saint never ceased to talk to his people about his departure that was to be soon. He did so with all the tenderness of love as he had always done before. 'Know ye, brethren,' he said, 'that as the sons of Israel were rescued from the land of Egypt so all people of this land will surely be freed from the unjust rule of the barbarians. They all, with their property, will leave these towns and go to the Roman province without falling into captivity. (5) But remember the command of the holy patriarch Joseph, whose name I, unworthy and lowly, invoke in making this request: "God will visit you; and ye shall carry my bones from here with you."[38] It is not for my benefit

---

38 Gen. 50.25 *(Vetus Latina)*.

but for yours. These places, now crowded with people, will be turned into such a desolation that the enemy, expecting to find some gold, will even break open the tombs of the dead.' (6) The truth of this prophecy was proved by the events of recent times. The command, however, that his body[39] should be removed was given by the most holy father with pious forethought for this reason, that when it would come to the general migration of the populace, the congregation of the brethren whom he had brought together should depart undivided and, having before them his memory, should remain united in one bond of holy fellowship.

41 (1) The day, too, on which blessed Severin was to leave his body for another world was indicated by him two or more years before in the following way. On the day of Epiphany, when St. Lucillus, the priest, had told him with an important air that on the following day he was going to celebrate the burial day of his abbot, St. Valentine, late bishop of the Raetiae, the servant of God made this reply: 'If blessed Valentine has entrusted you with the celebration of these solemn observances I also, being about to leave my body, bequeath to you the diligent observance of my vigil.' (2) When the latter, frightened by these words, suggested that it was rather he himself, a person frail with age, who would leave this world first, Severin went on to say: 'This, my holy priest, will be as you have heard; what has been laid down by the Lord will not be by-passed by the will of man.'

42 (1) Now Ferderuchus had received from his brother, Feva, king of the Rugi, one of the few towns that had remained on the bank of the Danube, namely, Favianis, beside

---

39 *Corpusculum*, in Late Latin a technical term for 'corpse' (*Thes. Ling. Lat.* 4. 1026.36-43), is used of the saint's dead body here, cf. Chapters 40 and 44.7; 45.1; 46.1. Characteristically, the dying Severin is said to have crossed his *corpus* (43.8). In a different sense, *corpus* is used of the saint's body as a relic, in connection with a miracle (46.4 twice). Pellegrino's interpretation (p. 16 and n. 33) 'miserable body' (cf. the use of the Greek diminutive *somátion*, especially in the writings of the Stoics) would suit the context here, but not so well in the other passages referred to.

which, as I have related, St. Severin dwelt. When Ferderuchus, as was his custom, went to greet him, the soldier of Christ began to talk to him about his journey more emphatically, and adjured him with these words: 'Know,' he said, 'that I shall soon go to my Lord. Therefore, I warn you, take care not to try, after my departure, to lay hands on anything that is under my trust, or to touch the livelihood of the poor and the captives. If you dare any such thing, which heaven forbid, you will feel the wrath of God.' (2) Ferderuchus, embarrassed by this unexpected admonition, said: 'Why must I be confounded by these adjuring words? I have no wish to deprive myself of such a great protection. Your holy generosity demands of me to add something to it, not to take anything away, in order that I, like my father, Flaccitheus, may be found worthy to be protected by your prayers. He certainly had learnt by experience that he was always assisted by the merits of your sanctity.' And Severin said: 'On the very first opportunity, you will want to violate my monastery, and then, at once, you will experience the truth of my words, and in the future, you will suffer the punishment—which I do not wish for you.' (3) Ferderuchus then promised to heed the warnings of the servant of Christ, and went home. The gentle teacher, never too tired to address his pupils, from time to time said: 'I confidently expect of the grace of my Lord Jesus Christ that, if you persevere in His work and remain peacefully united in my memory, He will give you the riches of eternal life and will not deny you the consolations of the present world.'

43 (1) On the fifth of January, he began to suffer slightly of a pain in his side. This lasted for three days; then, in the middle of the night, he asked the brethren to be with him. He gave them instructions concerning his body, and strengthened them with fatherly teaching in such words as these: (2) 'My most beloved sons in Christ, you know that when blessed Jacob[40] was about to leave the world and felt his death near,

---
40 Gen. 49.1-33.

he bade his sons to be with him, and rewarding every one of them with words of prophecy and blessing, revealed the secret mysteries that were to come. We, frail and lukewarm of heart, and left far behind by such great piety, dare not claim the same privilege for our feeble powers; yet one thing, which goes with humility, I shall not hide in silence, namely, to refer you to the example of the elders, whose death you should contemplate,[41] and whose pious way of life you should take as your model. When Abraham was called by the Lord, he obeyed in blind faith, willing to go to the place which he was to receive into his possession, and he went, not knowing where he was to go.[42] (3) Imitate the faith of this holy patriarch, imitate his sanctity, despise all that is earthly, always seek the home that is in heaven. I trust in the Lord that, for your sake, I shall reap eternal gain. I see that you have increased my joy by your spiritual fervor, that you love justice, that you gladly accept the bonds of brotherly love, that you strive for chastity, that you observe the rule of humility. These things, as far as a man can see them, I confidently praise and approve. (4) But pray that what is worthy in the eyes of men may be confirmed by the searching of eternal wisdom, for God does not see as man sees. He, as the word of God tells us,[43] "searches the hearts of all" and understands all the imaginations of the thought. Hope, therefore, by the help of constant prayer, that God may illumine the eyes of your hearts and, as blessed Eliseus wished,[44] may open them so that you may be able to understand how great is the help of the saints by whom we are protected on all sides, what great assistance is in readiness for the faithful. For our God comes near to the simple. (5) Those who fight for God should never be without much prayer. He who has not been ashamed to commit sin should not disdain to do penance. Do not hesi-

---

41 Cf. Heb. 13.7.
42 Cf. Heb. 11.8.
43 Rom. 8.27 (1 Par. 28.9).
44 Eliscus, i.e., Elisha: 4 Kings 6.17.

tate to weep over sinners if, perhaps, the divine wrath may be appeased by the flood of your tears, for He has seen fit to call a contrite spirit His sacrifice.[45] Let us be humble of heart, calm in mind, careful to avoid all sin, and always mindful of the precepts of God, knowing that our humble clothes, our name of monk, our title of religious vocation, our manifestation of piety will be of no avail if we are found to be degenerate and reproachable about our observance of the commandments. (6) Let, therefore, my beloved sons, your way of life be in harmony with your resolution. It is a great crime to follow the path of sin even for a man of the world. How far more so for monks, who flee from the lures of the world as if it were a wild beast, who have preferred Christ to all desires, whose gait and garment is supposed to be a proof of virtue? But why do I keep you, beloved sons, any further with my lengthy speech? (7) All that remains is to bid you a last farewell with the words of the Apostle, who says: "And now I commend you to God, and to the word of His grace, who is able to preserve you and to give you the inheritance among all the sanctified."[46] To Him be glory forever and ever, Amen.' (8) After this edifying address, he bade them all, one after the other, come along for a kiss. He received the sacrament of the communion; then he forbade them to weep for him; and making the sign of the cross over his whole body with his outstretched hand, he told them to sing psalms. When, overwhelmed with grief, they hesitated, he himself began to sing the psalm: 'Praise ye the Lord in His saints, let everything that breathes praise the Lord.'[47] (9) We had hardly answered the versicle when, on the eighth of January, he died

---

45 Ps. 50.19.
46 Acts 20.32. *Et nunc commendo vos Deo et verbo gratiae eius qui potens est conservare vos et dare hereditatem in omnibus sanctificatis.* (The variant readings *consolari* M, *sanctitatis* A, are not biblical variants.) Dom Chapman, p. 40, points out that Eugippius alone has *conservare* for *aedificare* and *in omnibus sanctificatis* (*in sanctificationibus* D, *in sanctificatis omnibus* cett.), and *eius* for *ipsius* with *e gig Hier.* Eugippius probably quotes from memory.
47 Ps. 150.1, 6

in the Lord. When he was buried, our elders, believing firmly that what he had said about our emigration, as many other things, would not remain unfulfilled, had a coffin made of wood so that his prophetic commands could be carried out when the time of the migration would come as it had been foretold.

44 (1) Ferderuchus, poor and godless, growing wilder and wilder in savage greed, had hardly heard of the death of blessed Severin when he decided to carry away the clothes destined for the poor and some other goods. And, adding sacrilege to this crime, he ordered a silver chalice and the other objects for the service of the altar to be likewise taken. (2) As these objects were standing on the altar, the steward who had been sent to commit this horrible deed did not dare to touch them; the king, therefore, compelled a soldier named Avitianus to seize the said things. The latter carried out his orders, though against his will; soon afterwards, however, he was unceasingly tormented by a trembling of all his limbs, and was also possessed by a demon. So he quickly changed his mind for the better and made up for his error. He took the holy vows and, changing his service, he took up heavenly arms and lived in the solitude of an island.[48] (3) Ferderuchus, however, forgetting the adjuration and prophecy of the holy man, did not leave the monastery before he had stripped it of everything except the walls, which he was unable to ship across the Danube. But soon the vengeance which had been predicted descended upon him: within a month's time, he was killed by Fredericus, his brother's son, and lost his spoils together with his life. (4) For this reason, Odovacar declared war on the Rugi. They were defeated, and Fredericus took to flight; his father, Feva, was taken prisoner, and he and his wicked wife were brought to Italy. Later, when

---

[48] Islands were favorite retreats of hermits and monks. Schuster, p. 190, refers to Capraria and Gorgon in the Tyrrhene Sea, which are known from Rutilius Namatianus; in Severin's time Lérins had already become famous.

Odovacar heard that Fredericus had returned to his kingdom, he at once sent his brother, Onoulf, with a great army; before him Fredericus flew again, and went to king Theoderic, who was then at the city of Novae in the province of Moesia. (5) Onoulf, however, acting on his brother's instructions, ordered all the Romans to emigrate to Italy. Then the whole population, freed of a life that was daily threatened by the robbery of the barbarians—the house, as it were, of Egyptian servitude—recognized the prophecies of St. Severin. Lucillus, who was then our venerable priest, had not forgotten the saint's command. When Count Pierius announced that all had to leave Lucillus, after the recitation of the evening psalms together with his monks, had the saint's burial place opened. (6) When it was opened, a scent of such great sweetness[49] came out of it that we all who had been standing around fell on the ground overwhelmed with joy and admiration. Then, contrary to what we expected as in the nature of things, namely, to find the limbs of his body disjointed—for five years had elapsed since he had been buried—we found the body whole and intact. For this miracle, we rendered great thanks to the Creator of all: that the saint's body, on which there had been no spices, which had not been treated by anyone, and even his beard and hair had, until then, remained intact. (7) We changed the linen, and then placed the body in the coffin which had long been prepared. It was put on a cart drawn by horses, and without delay moved off. We, and all the people of our province, who had to leave the towns on the bank of the Danube and were to be distributed over various parts of Italy,[50] went the same way. The saint's body was finally brought to a fort named Mount Feleter in the district of . . . .[51]

---

49 Sweet scent coming out of graves is a hagiographical commonplace; cf. H. Günter, *Psychologie der Legende*, (Freiburg 1949), 69; 112; *al.*
50 *Sortiti sunt sedes.* The word *sortiri* at that time need not imply that the distribution was made by lot, cf. Dopsch, p. 142.
51 The reconstructed manuscript reading *Mulsemensis regionis* (cf. Vetter, Noll[2], pp. 31f.) cannot be identified with any known district. No satisfactory emendation has so far been found.

45 (1) Then many people suffering from various diseases and others possessed by impure spirits quickly felt the remedy of divine grace. At that time, a dumb man was brought to the fort by his merciful relatives. He eagerly went to the oratory where the saint's body was still resting, and under it, his mouth being closed, he prayed in the chamber of his heart. Suddenly, his tongue was freed in the middle of his prayer and he praised God aloud. (2) When he returned to the inn where he used to stay and was, as usually, asked questions by nods and signs, he answered with a clear voice that he had prayed aloud and offered praise to God. When those who knew him heard him speak, they were struck with awe; they hurried to the oratory with shouting, and told the story to the priest, Lucillus, and to us who were with him and did not yet know what had happened. We all then greatly rejoiced in the divine mercy and rendered thanks.

46 (1) A noble lady, Barbaria, who, with her late husband, had known blessed Severin from hearsay and from letters, had a great devotion for him. When, after his death, she heard that the saint's body had been brought to Italy with great difficulty and that it had not yet been deposited in the earth, she invited our venerable priest, Marcianus, and the whole congregation by frequent letters. (2) Then, on the authority of holy Gelasius, pontiff of the Roman see, and with all the 492-496 people of Naples coming forth with reverence to join the funeral procession, the body was solemnly deposited at Castellum Lucullanum by bishop Victor, in a monument which ca. 492-498 the said lady had built. (3) During this solemn function, many persons, suffering from various ailments, whom it would be long to enumerate, at once found their health. Among these was a venerable maid of God, Processa by name, a citizen of Naples. Suffering severely from a troublesome sickness, she felt the call of the miracles of the holy body; she quickly went on her way, and as soon as she had walked under the vehicle on which the venerable body was carried, she was suddenly freed of all the pains of her limbs. (4) Laudicius, a blind man, hearing to his surprise the voices of the people singing psalms, asked anxiously what was going on. They replied that the body of a certain saint, Severin, was passing along. Moved in his heart, he asked to be led to the window, where those who could see would be able to watch from a distance the psalm-singing crowd and the vehicle with the saint's body. He leaned on the window and prayed, and suddenly he saw, pointing out one by one all his acquaintances and neighbors. At this, all who had heard about it thanked God with joyful tears. (5) Marinus, too, precentor (or: choirmaster?) of the holy church of Naples, who after a terrible illness was unable to recover because of a continual headache, put his head under the vehicle, full of confidence, and soon rose up free from pain; in memory of this favor, he came to the place and offered the sacrifice to God with thanksgiving, as he had vowed, every year on the anniversary of the saint's deposition. (6) Although many people know more miracles, it may be sufficient to have reported these three out of an immense number of favors and miracles which occurred on Severin's arrival. A monastery was built in that place to the memory of the blessed man, and still exists; through his merits, many possessed by devils have been cured and persons suffering from various diseases have received and still receive healing through God's grace, to whom is honor and glory forever and ever, Amen.

Here, illustrious minister of Christ, you have a memorandum out of which, by your masterly treatment, you will make a profitable work.

TO THE PRIEST EUGIPPIUS, HIS HOLY AND EVER BELOVED LORD, PASCHASIUS THE DEACON[1]

(1) My beloved brother in Christ,
You measure us by your skill in eloquence and by the happiness of your leisure, and shut your eyes to the bitterness of the many pursuits of sinners; in doing so you inflict on me a loss of modesty by your loving contemplation. (2) You have sent me your memorandum. There is nothing that could be added to it by the eloquence of a learned man. You have compressed in a short compass a work worthy to be placed before the whole Church. You have made known truthfully the life and character of blessed Severin, who lived in the provinces bordering on the Pannoniae, and you have handed down to posterity the memory of the miracles which the power of God has worked through him and which will last for all time—the works of the pious cannot perish with their age. You have done this in such a way that all those to whom the reading of your report brings him can see him, as it were, present and, in some way, experience his company. (3) And, therefore, since you have told with greater simplicity, and explained more gracefully than I could do what you ask me to relate, I believe that nothing can be added to your work by our effort. There is one way, in which we write about things that we have merely been told; there is another, in which we make known our own experiences. It is the disciples that are best qualified to call attention to the virtues of their teachers, because in their case they are communicated by close and frequent contact. (4) Inspired by divine grace, you know

---

1 This letter, being a sort of 'foreword,' probably had its original place immediately after the Letter of Eugippius to Paschasius: Noll[2], p. 35.

what great stimulus the deeds of the saints can add to the improvement of the minds of good men, what great fervor they give them, what strength of purity they instill. On this matter, the widely known voice of apostolic authority says: 'Be a pattern to the flock,'[2] and blessed Paul exhorts Timothy: 'Be an example to the faithful.'[3] For this reason, the same apostle draws up a brief list of the just, beginning with Abel,[4] and goes on to relate the virtues of outstanding men. (5) Thus, also, that model of faith, Matathias,[5] already approaching his glorious death, left to his sons, as by heredity, the examples of the saints, in order that they, stimulated by their admirable struggle, might despise their own lives for the holy fervor of the eternal laws. Not in vain had the father's instruction been imparted to his children; the deeds of their elders bore so much fruit in them that, confessing openly their faith, they frightened armed princes, stormed the camps of the blasphemers, destroyed far and wide the cults and altars of the demons,[6] and, decorated with perennial crowns, they provided a civic crown[7] for their glorious country. (6) Therefore, we, too, rejoice as we see the spouse of Christ[8] being provided with ornaments by our brother's service—not because at any time, so I believe, will there be lacking the model of elders more famous than the living, but because it is fitting that the house of the great king should have the standards of many victories. For true virtue is not crowded out by a multitude of other virtues; on the contrary, it is so much enriched and proceeds better towards its aim.

---

2 1 Peter 5.3.
3 1 Tim. 4.12.
4 Heb. 11.
5 1 Mac. 2.49ff.
6 1 Mac. 3.8; 5.44,68; 10.83f.
7 The civic crown (*corona civica*) was a wreath of oak given to a Roman who had saved a fellow citizen's life in battle. Later this honor was bestowed also on persons who had saved the citizen body in a grave crisis (Cicero, Augustus). It is in this wider meaning that the metaphor must here be understood.
8 Apoc. 21.2, 9; cf. Luke 5.34f.

IN SANCTI SEVERINI

Canticum laudis Domino canentes
Hunc diem festum celebremus omnes,
Quo Severinus penetravit almus
  Celsa polorum.

Quis stylo dives modulansque plectro
Cuncta signorum replicare possit,
Que potens Christus studiis opimis
  Contulit eius?

Inclitus vates nimiumque felix,
Sepius cui Deus intimabat
Tunc ad oppressi populi salutem
  Multa futura.

Voce presaga laqueos latronum
Atque predonum machinas retexens
Valde tutabat monitis supernis
  Oppida fessa.

Dulce solamen miseris ministrans
Horridam pestem famis amputavit,
Barbara plures feritate victos
  Solvit ab hoste.

Magne confessor, humilis magister,
Tu quidem normam monachis dedisti,
Calle demonstrans sobrio sequaces
  Scandere celum.

ON THE DAY OF SAINT SEVERIN[1]

Singing a song of praise to the Lord,
Let us all celebrate this solemn day
On which blessed Severin reached
The heights of heaven.

Which master of the written word or which singer to the lyre
Could relate all of the miracles
Which Christ in His power granted
To His great zeal?

Great was the prophet and very happy indeed
To whom God often revealed
For the benefit of the people who were than oppressed
Many things of the future.

Undoing the tricks of robbers
And the traps of plunderers with his prophetic voice,
He mightily protected the weary cities
By warnings received from above.

He brought sweet comfort to the miserable,
He made an end to the terrible scourge of famine,
And many who were under the cruel yoke of barbarism
He freed from the enemy.

Great confessor, humble teacher,
Thou hast given thy monks a rule,
Pointing out to them a sober path along which
They might ascend to heaven.

---

[1] The translation, which makes no claim to a poetic rendering, follows the original, line by line, merely for the convenience of comparison.

In tuis sanctis manibus refulsit
Celitus lumen refluensque crevit
Ad tuos haustus olei liquamen
  Fontis ad instar.

Condolens cunctos inhopes fovebat,
Languidos sanans relevabat egros:
Omnis accedens salubrem medelam
  Sumsit ab illo.

Tuque Sylvinum loculo iacentem,
Fratribus coram, precibus peractis,
Morte devicta redire fecisti ad
  Gaudia vite.

Cereos flamma fidei cremante
Arguit sanctus pater infideles:
Moxque flammescunt deitatis igne
  Algida corda.

Cuius ad funus veniens sacratum
Mutus accepit modulos loquele,
Cecus exultat procul ambulantes
  Cernere notos.

Neapolis, gaude redimita festa,
Plaude celestem retinens patronum,
Quem tibi summus decus et iuvamen
  Prestitit auctor.

In thy holy hands there shone
Light from heaven, and flowing back to its source
When thou pouredst it out the liquor of oil increased
Like a fountain.

In his compassion he tended all the needy,
He brought relief to the sick by healing them;
All who came to him received from him
A salutary remedy.

When Silvinus was lying on his bier,
In the presence of his brethren, after prayers had been said,
Thou, defeating death, madest him come back
To the joys of life.

By the burning flame of faith
The holy father denounces the tapers of the infidels;
Soon are kindled by the fire of God
The cold hearts.

A dumb man coming to his holy funeral
Received the faculty of speech,
A blind man to his joy is able to see from a distance
His friends walking in the procession.

Naples, rejoice, adorned for the feast,
Clap hands in joy as thou holdest the heavenly patron
Whom thy Creator gave thee as a great ornament and help.

Huius o clemens meritis creator
Gloriam nobis veniamque confer,
Quo tui cultus super astra semper
   Luce fruamur.

Gloriam Patri resonemus omnes
Eius et Nato iubilemus apte,
Cum quibus regnat simul et Creator
   Spiritus almus.[2]

---

[2] The last three lines of this stanza, which in our MSS are not written out in full (a common practice with regard to doxologies) have been supplemented by Bulst (Edit. Heidelbergenses, p. 55) from a hymn on St. Laurence, ed. by Blume, *Analecta Hymnica* 51 (1908), nr. 172.

By his merits, o clement Creator,
Bestow on us glory and pardon,
That we may always be in the light of Thy service,
A light which obscures the stars.

Let us all sing glory to the Father,
Let us also praise joyfully His Son as is becoming,
And the Holy Spirit, who is King and Creator
Together with them.

EXCURSUS

FAVIANIS

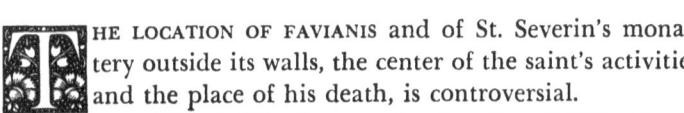HE LOCATION OF FAVIANIS and of St. Severin's monastery outside its walls, the center of the saint's activities and the place of his death, is controversial.

Mommsen (CIL 3.687; *Gesammelte Schriften* 7.521) identified Favianis with Mauer an der Url, south of the Danube, near Ybbs, where there are ruins of a Roman *castellum* and where a Roman brick (*tegula*) has been found which bears the stamp of the *legio prima Noricorum* (CIL 3.5756), a troup which was stationed at Favianis in late antiquity (cf. Notitia Dignitatum, occ. 34.41).

Friedrich Kenner[1] suggested that Favianis occupied the site of Mautern, further east, on the southern bank of the Danube opposite Krems. Excavations have proved that Mautern was a place of some importance in Roman times. It was a fortified locality with a military garrison and with a civilian population, both inside and outside its walls; there is also evidence of Christian worship. The Roman name of Mautern is not known on epigraphical or other documentary evidence. Kenner's identification, which won general acceptance, has been followed by us.

During the Middle Ages, from the tenth century onwards, and down to the age of the Baroque, Favianis was thought to be either identical with or to have been situated in the vicinity of Vienna (the Roman names of which were Vindobona, Vindomana, Vindomina); St. Severin's cell, the Burgum

---
1 Cf. in particular *Berichte und Mitteilungen des Altertums-Vereines zu Wien* 19 (1880) 49-104.

ad Vineas, was then located at Heiligenstadt (alias Heiligenstatt —*civitas sancta* or *locus sanctus* in medieval Latin documents), a western suburb of Vienna, in spite of its considerable distance from the ancient and medieval city—five miles, as against Eugippius' one. A cult of St. Severin at Heiligenstadt is attested since the sixteenth century; in the neighboring suburb of Sievering (often said to be a corruption of 'Severin,' though on linguistically doubtful grounds) his cult is, at least, as early as the fifteenth. The theory Favianis = Vienna played some role in the policy of the Babenberg family, margraves and later dukes of Ostarichi (Austria), in the twelfth century. The Austrian humanist, Wolfgang Lazius (16th century), relates a legend according to which margrave Leopold III (St. Leopold of Austria) used stones from St. Severin's cell at Heiligenstadt for the building of his monastic foundation, Klosterneuburg.

In the modified form that Favianis is actually Heiligenstadt, this theory was revived as a result of the discovery under the parish church of St. Jakob, Heiligenstadt, of a late-antique tomb which subsequently had been evacuated. These excavations were carried out in 1952 and 1953 by the parish priest, Rev. Klemens Kramert, and by Dr. A. Neumann, Director of the Römische Museum, Vienna. A full official report on the excavations has not yet been published; there are, however, some interim reports by Dr. Neumann in the *Wiener Amtsblatt*, a brief notice by Professor R. Egger,[2] two fuller reports by Dr. Neumann,[3] and a very detailed, but non-professional, account by K. Kramert (KW 1.13-36). Inspired by these excavations, an amateur study team under the leadership of Pfarrer Kramert and the late Dr. Ernst Karl Winter began to re-interpret the text of Eugippius and to re-examine all the other evidence relating to St. Severin, Roman Austria, Heiligenstadt-Sievering, etc. The views of this group, stated in great

---

[2] *Anzeiger der Österreichischen Akademie der Wissenschaften*, phil.-hist. Klasse, 1954, no. 21.
[3] *Archaeologia* 11 (1959-60) 46-50; *Bericht über den V. Internationalen Kongress für Vor- und Frühgeschichte, Hamburg 1958* (Berlin 1961) 604-608.

detail in a two-volume publication,[4] have come in for much criticism on the part of Austrian scholars.[5] This ingenious, but unconvincing, piece of special pleading would hardly deserve consideration here were it not for the fact that the same views have been expressed by Dr. Winter in an American periodical of high scholarly standing.[6] To argue with a writer whose reasoning is overtly aprioristic, not to say question-begging, would be useless. I shall, therefore, be content to state the relevant facts and to discuss briefly the conclusions to which they would seem to lend themselves.

The excavations at St. Jakob's have revealed, in chronological order, (1) a Roman building, probably some military object (depot or factory), in its renovated state not later than the fourth century A.D., which was subsequently converted in part to a non-military purpose; (2) within this structure, an empty tomb above the ground, of post-Valerian times (fifth century?), and a smaller structure of about the same period, which, having at first been tentatively described as a primitive baptismal fount, is now considered a child's grave by archaeologists; (3) remnants of a pre-romanesque church-building with an altar-stone above the adult's tomb.[7] Two stone bases of uncertain date might, in the opinion of Winter (KW 2.90f.), have supported a baldachin (*kiborion*) in early Byzantine times, but this is purely a matter of speculation. That the larger of the two late-antique tombs was the burial place of some important Christian personality is perhaps suggested by the fact that its location was apparently taken into account by the pre-romanesque altar and church, and also by the twelfth-century romanesque church, which is the nucleus of the present one.[8] The tomb was found empty, without any

---

4 Cf. Bibliography. A convenient summary can be found in the pamphlet by E. K. Winter, *Wo lag Favianis?* (Vienna 1957).
5 Bibliography of the controversy: KW 2.45f.
6 The Byzantine Millenium of Vienna, in *Medievalia et Humanistica* 10 (1956) 1-31.
7 This might have been the Carolingian church of St. Michael's (K. Lechner, *Wiener Geschichtsblätter* 68 [1953] 69).
8 However, Neumann (*Archaeologia* 11.50) points out that this might have been due to purely practical considerations.

human remains or traces of plundering. If it was used at the time of its erection, the body would have been lifted again on some later occasion. Kramert and Winter believe that this was done at the end of the Roman period; Dr. Neumann suggests that both tombs were evacuated by the Carolingian church-builders and that the remains were interred in the surrounding cemetery.

As regards the possibility that the larger tomb might have been the temporary resting place of St. Severin's body, archaeologists who took a part in or inspected the excavations have been very cautious and reserved in their pronouncements. At best, nothing more could be claimed for this tomb than that it fulfills certain conditions without which it would not qualify for the identification at all. For declaring it to be the tomb of St. Severin, far more specific indicia would be needed. In the absence of any epigraphical evidence *in situ*, it would be necessary to prove, independently of the excavation, that the identification of Favianis with Heiligenstadt is either certain or, at least, highly probable. In spite of the efforts of Dr. Winter and his team, such proof is entirely lacking.

For the location of Favianis, we possess the following indicia:

Favianis belonged to the province of Noricum Ripense; Vindobona (Vindomana, Vindomina) and its townland belonged to the province of Pannonia Superior or Pannonia Prima. The frontier between the two provinces was the Mons Cetius (Wienerwald with Kahlenberg), the northernmost part of the eastern Alps, which touches the Danube *west* of Heiligenstadt. The Vienna district was thus a border area, but it cannot be established (as Dr. Winter has endeavored to do) that this area was St. Severin's base of operations. Eugippius tells us that St. Severin came from the east *ad Norici Ripensis oppida Pannoniae superiori vicina* (Epist. Eugipp. 10), and his words are echoed by Paschasius (Epist. Pasch. 2): *Severini finitimas Pannoniorum* (i.e., *provinciae*) *provincias incolentis*, viz., the provinces bordering on the province of the Pannonii, that is,

Noricum Ripense and Rhaetia. In the *Commemoratorium* (1.1), Eugippius makes a statement to the same effect, though with less precision: Severin, coming from the east, *in vicinia Norici Ripensis et Pannoniorum parvo quod Asturis dicitur oppido morabatur*. It stands to reason that the slightly vaguer statement must be interpreted in the light of the more explicit one: Asturis, if correctly identified with Klosterneuburg, is situated near the border of Noricum and Pannonia, but just within the former, being the easternmost town of that province. Winter makes a great deal of the fact that the Anonymous Valesianus, an Italian chronicler of the sixth century, quotes (45) from Eugippius *in libris vitae beati Severini monachi intra Pannoniam*. There need be no contradiction, however, between this statement and the text of Eugippius, which the Anonymous had before him. The two Noric provinces belonged administratively to the *diocensis Pannoniarum* (*Laterculus Provinciarum Veronensis*, 4th century, p. 249, Seeck). Neither does the fact that, according to the Notitia Dignitatum (occ. 34, title), Pannonia Prima and Noricum Ripense were under the command of a single *dux* imply that the official frontier between the two provinces had become obsolete. In this very document, the specifications for the two provinces are kept strictly apart. As late as the eighth century, Paulus Diaconus, following Eugippius, states that St. Severin's monastery (*coenobium*) was *in Noricorum finibus* (*Historia Langobardorum* 1.19), and that Odoacer visited him there *dum adhuc* (on his way from Pannonia to Italy) *per Noricorum rura exercitum duceret* (*Historia miscellanea*, 15).[9] However unimportant, from a practical point of view, the frontier between the provinces may have become at a time

---

9 Otto of Freising, in the twelfth century, renders this passage as follows: *dum per inferiores Noricae partes vel superiorem Pannoniam transiret, virum Dei Severinum . . . adiit* (Chron. 4.30). Contrary to Winter (KW 2.266), I regard the words *vel superiorem Pannoniam* as a comment made by the chronicler. Being a son of Leopold III of Austria, Otto would be familiar with the equation, current in Babenberg circles (KW 2.267), of the *Marca Orientalis* ('Ostmark,' i.e., Austria) with the ancient Pannonia Superior.

when *confinia Danubii rebus turbabantur ambigus* (Eugippius, 1.1), there can be no doubt that it existed in theory, and there is no evidence to show that it had changed since the time of Diocletian. Insistence on this formal point may appear pedantic, but to give it up would mean to abandon one of the few positive criteria by which we can go.

Within Noricum Ripense, the location of Favianis can be circumscribed, if not exactly determined, by the following considerations. From Asturis, the easternmost town of the province, and thus the first one to be reached by a traveler coming from the east, Severin 'turned away' (*declinavit*, cf. p. 57, n. 2) to the *proximum oppidum* of Comagenis (1.3), and from there was called to Favianis. There is nothing to suggest that Severin went back in an eastern direction. As a matter of fact, if our interpretation of the evidence so far adduced is valid, there would, after the destruction of Asturis, be no room for another town inside Noricum to the east of Comagenis. And since a southern (inland) direction is excluded by the fact that Favianis was situated on or near the Danube (cf. 3.3; 8.2; 22.4; 23.1; 31.1; 42.1), it must be sought further to the west. On the other hand, it might be deduced from Notitia Dignitatum (occ. 34.41) that Favianis ('Fafianae') was located to the east of Adiuvense. Favianis would thus have been situated between Adiuvense (Ybbs) and Comagenis (Tulln). The only place that comes into consideration at all is Mautern.[10] The fact that two out of three *tegulae* with a stamp that seems to refer to the *numeri Noricorum*[11] were found at Mautern may be mentioned in support of this identification.[12]

---

10 In Mauer an der Url (Mommsen's original identification, cf. above, p. 111), apart from its location west of the Ybbs, there is no evidence of either a one-time civilian population or Christian cult. Besides, this place is rather too far away from the Danube to answer Eugippius' description. Mauer might be the *Lacus Felicis* of Notitia Dignitatum (occ. 34.33); *Itinerarium Antonini* 234.4; 248.6.
11 Cf. R. Egger, *Anzeiger der Osterr. Akademie der Wiss.*, phil.-hist. Klasse, 1954, 108-110. Winter's criticism of Egger, KW 2.169-172, is based largely on a misunderstanding of the latter's argument.
12 Against Winter's revival of the view that Mautern is the Roman Cetium, cf. above, p. 14, n. 8.

Another detail is embarrassing rather than helpful. Eugippius tells (22.4) of Severin's journey by boat from Batavis to Favianis, *quod centum et ultra milibus* (over 100 Roman miles = over 150 km) *aberat*. According to the present course of the Danube, the waterway distance between Passau and Krems (opposite Mautern), as shown in the timetable of the Donau-Dampfschiffahrts-Gessellschaft, is 224 km, or 149 Roman miles.[13] However, a further journey on the river from Mautern to Heiligenstadt would have to cover another 68 km (46 Roman miles).[14] If Eugippius' figure is grossly inaccurate, the identification Favianis = Heiligenstadt would almost double the margin of his inaccuracy.

Inconclusive for the location of Favianis is the fact, implied in the *Commemoratorium* (ch. 9), that the Rugi had their royal seat opposite that town across the Danube. Archaeology has, so far, not succeeded in locating the Rugian residence. On general grounds, one would not look for it on the periphery of their territory, that is, at the Bisamberg (opposite Klosterneuburg), as the Heiligenstadt theory requires. The Rugi would naturally have coveted the fertile plain of the Marchfeld to the east of that mountain, but this proves nothing for the location of their royal seat.[15] It is far more likely that

---

13 A similar, and even worse, inaccuracy is found in 24.1, where Ioviaco is said to be *viginti et amplius a Batavis milibus disparatum*. According to the *Itinerarium Antonini*, whose figures in this section Mommsen has found 'detailed and accurate' (*plenos et probos*, CIL 3.687), the distance (by road) is 38 Roman miles, and would be even more on the waterway. (On the assumption that Ioviaco is Aschach, the distance would be 66 km = 44 Roman miles.)
14 Noll[2], p. 134, suggests that no accurate figure was intended.
15 Another of Winter's arguments is equally indecisive. He deduces a gravitation of Rugian power towards the east from the hostility shown to them by the Ostrogoths of Pannonia (Eugippius, ch. 5). Eugippius says that the Goths threatened the Rugi *ex inferiore Pannonia* and denied them transit to Italy (obviously by the age-old route along the eastern edge of the Alps). It matters little for our problem whether Eugippius actually means the Roman province of Pannonia Inferior or, in non-technical language, refers to the remoter districts of Pannonia Superior, between the Scarniunga River and the Lacus Pelsois (Plattensee), where they had settled after their victory over Attila's sons (Iordanes, *Getica* 268). There certainly is no evidence to show that they held the province in an organized manner or that (as Winter thinks) they had established a permanent foothold at Vindomana.

the Rugian kings resided at the foot of the Mannhartsberg, which stretches from Krems northwards towards the Moravian frontier. However, in this matter it seems impossible to go beyond general probability. Unlike Favianis, Heiligenstadt was not a place of any importance in Roman times. Winter's suggestion that, as an emergency measure, a small and not very compact settlement was made the seat of military and civil authorities and was given some sort of status (KW 1.115; 2.174, and elsewhere) is unsupported by evidence of any kind.[16] Eugippius' numerous references to Favianis as a *civitas* (3.1; 4.6; cf. *civitatula*, ch. 3—hardly an argument in Winter's favor) or an *oppidum* (4.5,6; 22.4; 31.1; 42.1) and to its walls (4.1,) differ in no way from those to such long-established towns as Batavis or Lauriacum.

This is the evidence. The arguments for identifying Favianis with Mautern are, admittedly, not cogent,[17] but the balance of probability is decidedly in its favor. The story behind the tomb under St. Jakob's is lost. A continuity of pious devotion, if not of worship, in that place is probable (though not demonstrable), but we have no means of determining its object. The mere fact that it was a Christian burial place would be sufficient for qualifying it as *locus sanctus*. That it should, centuries later, have attracted the name of the Apostle of Noricum, the only great name of Christian antiquity that was remembered (or rather rediscovered), need cause no surprise. To simplify history in such a way is characteristic of the popular mind. Neither can the Babenberg rulers be blamed for

---

They would, all the same, be able to control the route to Italy and to make forays into Noricum and across the Danube (Eugippius 5.3).

16 Winter (KW 2.105) assumes a 'transmigration' of the Celto-Roman population from Vindomina to Favianis-Heiligenstadt, following upon an earlier one from Carnuntum to Vindomina. The latter, however, is merely read by him into a note in the Notitia Dignitatum (occ. 34.28), which, if trustworthy, refers only to the transfer of the river flotilla (*classis Histrica*).

17 I am not quite as pessimistic, though, as is H. Löwe, Wattenbach-Levison 1.46, who terms Favianis 'a locality which has disappeared without leaving a trace.'

taking up, apparently in good faith, what, by their time, may well have become an established tradition. These, however, are no foundations for the historian to build upon.

INDICES

GENERAL INDEX[1]

Abel, Epist. Pasch. 4.
Abraham, 43.2.
Aenus, *see* Inn.
Alamanni: often raid Batavis, 19.1; raid Quintanis, 27.1; defeated by the people of Quintanis, 27.2; devastate Noricum, 25.3; further invasions feared by king Feva, 31.4.
Alps: miraculously crossed in mid-winter, ch. 29. (The Roman road led from Tiburnia through the Lieser valley and northwards, probably across the Radstädter Pass, cf. Noll, p. 179.)
Amantius, deacon, Severin's messenger to king Gibuld, 19.3.
Ambrose, St., bishop of Milan (ca. 340-397), his authority invoked, 36.2.
Ambrosius, exiled, called back by Odovacar at Severin's request, 32.1.
Ariminum (Rimini), the monk Bassus lived near A., Epist. Eugipp. 1.
Asturis (Klosterneuburg or, p o s s i b l y, Zeiselmauer), place of Severin's first public appearance in Noricum, 1.1; destroyed, 1.5.
Attila, king of the Huns, dies, 1.1.
Avitianus, soldier in the service of Ferderuchus, his crime and penance, 44.2.

Barbaria, an Italian lady,[2] offers a burial place for St. Severin, 46.1.
Bassus, a monk of saintly reputation, Epist. Eugipp. 1.
Batavis (formerly Castra Batava, named after the Batavi on the lower Rhine,

---
1 Cf. now also Gertrud Pascher, *Römische Siedlungen und Strassen im Limesgebiet zwischen Enns und Leitha* (Der römische Limes in Österreich, Heft 19, Vienna 1949), esp. cols. 63f. (Klosterneuburg—Asturis), 85-90 (Mautern—Favianis), and 153-155 (Tulln—Comagenis). This publication is equally important for its source material (inscriptions, reports on excavations) as for its bibliographical references.
2 Winter (KW 2.63) suggests that she might have been the widow of Orestes (Epist. Eugipp. 8).

from whom its garrison was originally recruited; now Passau), between **Danube** and **Inn**, often raided by the Alamanni, 19.1; its Roman garrison the last to hold out, 20.1; raided by Hunumund, 22.4,5; the people of Quintanis retreat to Batavis, 27.1; taken by the Thoringi, 27.3. Cf. 22.1; 24.1.

Boiotro (originally, after the Celtic settlement, Boiodurum; now Innstadt), near Batavis, on the eastern (Norican) bank of the Inn, 22.1; cf. 36.1.

Bonosus, one of Severin's monks, of 'barbarian' race, ch. 35.

Burgum, near Favianis, place of Severin's retreat, 4.7.

Businca (now 'Kalter Bach'?), a small tributary of the Danube, at Quintanis, 15.1.

Christ, Jesus Christ, *passim*.

Comagenis (Tulln), held by barbarians under treaty, 1.3,4; freed, 1.5; 2.1,2; cf. 3.1; visited by Severin again, ch. 33.

Constantius, pontiff of Lauriacum, 30.2; cf. Ennodius, *Vita s. Antonii* 10.

Cucullis (Kuchl, south of Salzburg), Roman fort, 11.2; pagan rites still performed there, 11.2-5; locusts destroy crops, ch. 12.

Danube (Danuvius; once, 10.2, named Hister); frontier between Romans and Rugians, 31.1; Romans forcibly transported across the Danube, 8.2; 10.1; D. as waterway, 22.4; crossed, 9.1; 10.2; 23.1; 33.1; floods Quintanis, 15.1; heavily frozen, 4.10; cf. 1.1; 3.2,3; 19.1; 28.1; 42.1; 44.3,7.

Deogratias, bearer of Eugippius' letter to Paschasius, Epist. Eugipp. 6.

East: Severin had been a monk in the East, Epist. Eugipp. 10; *Commemoratorium* 1.1.

Egypt: sons of Israel leaving Egypt, 40.4; cf. 44.5.

Eliseus, the prophet: 28.5 (oil miracle) ; 43.4.

Eugippius, priest, disciple of St. Severin: Epist. Eugipp. (title) ; Epist. Pasch. (title).

Favianis (Mautern),[3] freed from famine, ch. 3; from brigands, 4.1-4; paying tribute to the Rugi, bordering on their territory, 31.1; cf. 8.2; falls to Ferderuchus, 42.1; Severin's monastery near Favianis, 4.6,7; 10.1;

---
3 On the identification of Favianis, c.f Excursus, p. 111ff.

INDEX

22.4; 23.1; 31.6; *see* p. 111.
Feba, *see* Feva.
Feletheus, *see* Feva.
(Mons) Feleter (also Mons Feretrus, Mons Feretratus; now San Leo at Monte Feltre, near San Marino in Umbria: cf. Mommsen, *Gesammelte Schriften* 7 [1909] 529), temporary resting place of St. Severin's body, 44.7.
Ferderuchus, brother of Feva, obtains Favianis, 42.1; admonished by Severin, 42.1-3; loots Severin's monastery after the saint's death, 44.1-3.
Feva (Feba, Feletheus), king of the Rugi, 8.1; 42.8; to be asked for a trading license, 22.2; wishes to settle Romans in his towns, 31.1-6; admonished by the dying Severin, 40.1-3; taken prisoner by Odovacar, 44.4.
Flaccitheus, king of the Rugi, father of Feva and Ferderuchus, threatened by the Goths, counseled by Severin, ch. 5; cf. 8.1; 42.2.[4]
Fredericus, son of Feva, held as hostage by the king's goldsmiths, 8.3; kills Ferderuchus, 44.3; defeated by Odovacar and his brother, Onoulf, flees to Theoderic, 44.4.
Gelasius, pope (492-496), authorizes Severin's burial at Castellum Lucullanum, 46.2.
Gervasius and Protasius, SS., martyrs, patrons of Milan, where, according to their legend, they were put to death during the war against the Marcomanni. Their relics were discovered and lifted by St. Ambrose. Feast: June 18. Some relics of G. and P. acquired by Severin, 9.3.
Gibuld, king of the Alamanni, his dealings with Severin, ch. 19.
Giso, Feva's queen, opposes Severin, 8.1ff.; admonished by Severin, 40.1-3.
Goths refuse Flaccitheus passage through Noricum Mediterraneum, 5.1; their hostility to the Rugi, 5.2; besiege Tiburnia, 17.4.
Heruli, destroy Ioviaco, 24.3.

---

[4] Pedigree of the Rugian dynasty:

```
              Flaccitheus
              (d. ca. 475)
              ╱         ╲
Giso—Feva (Feletheus)   Ferderuchus
    (ca. 475-487)         (d. 482)
         │
     Fredericus
```

Hister, *see* Danube.
Huns, 1.1.
Hunumundus, captures Batavis, 22.4. His alleged identity with Hunimundus (so some MSS), king of the Suebi (Iordanis, *Hist. Gothorum* 53ff.) cannot be proved.

Inn (Aenus), tributary of the Danube, joining the latter at Batavis, 19.1; boats icebound on Inn, 3.3; basilica of Boiotro across the Inn, 22.1.
Inportunus, consul a. 509, Epist. Eugipp. 1.
Ioviaco (of uncertain location, between Engelhartszell and Aschach, on the Danube), 24.1. (Tentatively identified with Eferding by Bulst, Edit. Heidelbergenses, p. 57.) *See* Excursus, p. 111.
Israelites, 40.4.
Italy: Flaccitheus intends to go to Italy, 5.1; Odovacar on his way to Italy visits Severin, 7.1; cf. 6.6; pay of garrison at Batavis to be fetched from Italy, 20.1; Feva taken to Italy as prisoner, 52.4; the Romans of Noricum Ripense evacuated to Italy, 44.5,7; Severin's body taken to Italy, 44.7-46 ex.
Iuvao (more commonly Iuvavum, now Salzburg) 13.1.

Jacob, the patriarch, 43.2.
James, St., apostle, 30.5.
Jesus, *see* Christ.
John the Baptist, his relics, 22.1; 23.2.
Joseph, the patriarch, 40.5.

Latin: Severin a true Latin (*homo omnino Latinus*), Epist. Eugipp. 10.
Laudicius, a blind man healed at Severin's funeral, 46.4.
Lauriacum (Lorch near the Enns), 18.1; inhabitants of Batavis emigrate to L., 27.2; 28.1; 31.1; cf. 6; saved from an attempted barbarian attack, ch. 30.[5]
Lot's wife, 9.4.
Lucania, the monk Bassus died in L., Epist. Eugipp. 1.
Lucillus, priest, recovers captives from the Alamanni, 19.5; Severin foretells him the day of his death, 41.1,2; directs the exhumation of Severin's body, 44.5; cf. 45.2.
Lucullanum castellum, near Naples (now Pizzofalcone), burial place of St. Severin, 46.2. The *castellum* was

---

[5] On Lauriacum, cf. now *Forschungen in Lauriacum*, vol. 1: *Die Versuchsgrabungen des Jahres 1951, Forschungsbericht 1950-51* (Linz 1953).

named after the gardens and fishponds of Lucullus (d. ca. 57 B.C.). It was also the place of exile of the last Roman emperor, Romulus Augustulus.

Mamertinus, tribune (commander) of Favianis, afterwards bishop (there?) 4.2.
Marcianus, citizen of Cucullis, afterwards priest, 11.2; monk under Severin, and his successor, 37.1; evades the barbarians, 37.2; invited, as head of the community, by Barbaria, 46.1.
Marcus, subdeacon, witnesses a miracle of St. Severin, 16.6.
Marinus, 'head of the singers' of the Church of Naples, healed at Severin's funeral, 46.5.
Matathias, the high priest, Epist. Pasch. 5.
Maternus, *ostiarius* of Quintanis, 16.2,6.
Maurus, janitor of Severin's monastery, 10.1,2.
Maximianus, priest of Ioviaco 24.2.
Maximus, citizen of Noricum, brings Severin's message to Paulinus, 25.1; leader of a convoy of supplies for Severin's poor, 29.1.
Milan: a leper from the territory of M. travels to Severin, 26.1; St. Ambrose, bishop of M., 36.2.
Moderatus, chanter, 24.1.
Moesia, province of, held by Theoderic, 44.4.
Mons Feleter, *see* Feleter.

Naples, 46.2,5.
Noricum (always meaning Noricum Mediterraneum, cf. Robinson, p. 65, n. 1): Severin's letters to N., 17.4; 25.1,2; Paulinus, bishop of N., 21.2; 25.2; convoy from N., ch. 29; cf. 37.1.
Noricum Ripense, Epist. Eugipp. 10; *Commonitorium* 1.1; its upper towns, 11.1.
Novae, city of Moesia (Sistow in Bulgaria), Theoderic's residence, 44.4.

Odovacar, of the tribe of the Sciri, seeks Severin's blessing, is foretold by him his future greatness, 7.1; recalls the exiled Ambrosius, 32.1; Severin's prophecy about the duration of his reign, 32.2; his war with the Rugi, 44.4; orders the Romans of Noricum to be settled in Italy, 44.5.
Onoulf (Hunwulf), brother of Odovacar, 44.4,5.
Orestes, patrician, Epist. Eugipp. 8. He was a Pan-

nonian, secretary to Attila; after the latter's death, he returned to the Roman Empire. The title *patricius* (at that time a distinction conferred by the emperor) was given him in 475 as commander-in-chief of the Roman army. He had his minor son, Romulus Augustulus, proclaimed emperor in the same year. He was killed when Odovacar came to power in 476.

Pannonia, Upper, Epist. Eugipp. 10; Goths in Lower Pannonia, 5.1; both Pannonias in a state of unrest after Attila's death, 1.1. Cf. Epist. Pasch. 2.

Paschasius, deacon, Epist. Eugipp. (title); Epist. Pasch. (title); *see* Introduction, p. 6.

Paul, the apostle, Epist. Pasch. 4.

Paulinus, priest, afterwards bishop of Noricum: Severin's prophecy about his election, ch. 21; receives letters of warning from Severin, 25.1,2.

Pientissimus, assistant of Severin, 28.4.

Pierius, count, orders Romans to vacate Noricum, 44.5. He died in 490, during the struggle between Odovacar and Theoderic.

Postumianus (partner in the first Dialogue of Sulpicius Severus), 36.3.

Primenius, priest from Italy, friend of Orestes, asks Severin about his birthplace, Epist. Eugipp. 7.

Processa (nun?), citizen of Naples, healed, 46.3.

Procula, widow of Favianis, hoards grain, 3.2.

Protasius, martyr, *see* Gervasius.

Quintanis (probably Künzing) and its suspended church, ch. 15; its inhabitants emigrate to Batavis, 27.1; cf. 24.2.

Raetiae, 3.3; Valentinus, bishop of R., 41.1; Raetiae Secundae, 15.1.

Renatus, one of Severin's monks, 37.1.

Romans, i.e., the Celto-Romans of Noricum, *passim*.

Rugi, a Germanic tribe, temporarily settled north of the Danube, *passim*.

Severin, *passim*; *see* chapter headings, pp. 51 ff.

Severus Sulpicius, quoted, 36.3. On this writer, cf. B. M. Peebles, Fathers of the Church, vol. 7 (1949) 79-100.

Silvinus, priest of Quintanis, recalled from death, ch. 16.
Stilicho (Vandal, general and minister of the emperor Honorius, d. 408), 36.2.
Sulpicius, *see* Severus.

Teio, leper, healed by Severin, ch. 34.
Theoderic, leader of the Ostrogoths, in Moesia, afterwards ruler of Italy, 44.4.
Thoringi, a Germanic tribe, invade Batavis, 27.3; threaten Noricum, 31.4.
Tiburnia (elsewhere always Teurnia; now St. Peter im Holz, in Carinthia), metropole of Noricum, 21.2; besieged by the Goths, 17.4. Its importance as a political and ecclesiastical center dates from the fourth century.
Tiguntia, a brook of uncertain identification, near Favianis, 4.4.
Timotheus, St. Paul's Epistle to him, Epist. Pasch. 4.
Titas, mountain near Ariminum (the Monte Titano of San Marino), Epist. Eugipp. 1.

Ursus, monk of Severin, healed of a deadly pustule, ch. 38.

Valens, one of Severin's monks, 30.2.
Valentinus, bishop of Raetiae 41.1. (Cf. *Bibliotheca Hagiographica Latina*, no. 8462; however, Noll,[2] p. 141, doubts the identification.)
Victor, bishop of Naples (ca. 492-498), buries Severin, 46.3.
Vineyards, at the place of Severin's retreat, off Favianis, 4.6.

INDEX OF HOLY SCRIPTURE

(Books of the Old Testament)

Genesis 19.26: 9.4; 49.1-33: 43.2; 50.25: 40.5.
Exodus 14.14: 4.3.
Deuteronomy 32.13: Ep. Eug. 3.
4 Kings 4.2-7: 28.5; 6.17: 43.4.
1 Paralipomenon 28.9: 43.4.
Psalm 50.19: 43.5; 112.2: 23.1, 28.3, 29.4; 150.1,6: 43.8.
Joel 2.12,15: 12.2.
Jeremia 17.5: 5.2.
1 Machabees 2.49ff., 3.8, 5.44, 68, 10.83 f.: Ep. Pasch. 5.

(Books of the New Testament)

Matthew 5.14f.: 4.8; 6.3: Ep. Eug. 9, 28.3; 15.42: 3.2; 20.28: 28.3; 25.33: Ep. Eug. 9.
Mark 10.45: 28.3.
Luke 5.34f.: Ep. Pasch. 6; 17.32: 9.4.
Acts 20.32: 43.7.
Romans 8.27: 43.4.
1 Corinthians 2.13: Ep. Eug. 3; 5.5: 36.2; 7.25: 6.2.
Ephesians 1.4: 4.11; 5.5: 3.2.
1 Timothy 2.2: 1.1; 4.12: Ep. Pasch. 4.
Hebrews 11: Ep. Pasch. 4; 11.8, 13.7: 43.2.
James 5.16: 30.5.
1 Peter 5.3: Ep. Pasch. 4.
Apocalypse 21.2,9: Ep. Pasch. 6.

NON-BIBLICAL QUOTATIONS

Athanasius, *Vita s. Antonii* c. 20: 9.4.
Paulinus, *Vita s. Ambrosii* c. 43: 36.2.
Sulpicius Severus, *Dialogi* 1.20.7: **36.3.**

THE FATHERS OF THE CHURCH SERIES

(A series of approximately 100 volumes when completed)

VOL. 1: THE APOSTOLIC FATHERS (1947)
 LETTER OF ST. CLEMENT OF ROME TO THE CORINTHIANS (trans. by Glimm)
 THE SO-CALLED SECOND LETTER (trans. by Glimm)
 LETTERS OF ST. IGNATIUS OF ANTIOCH (trans. by Walsh)
 LETTER OF ST. POLYCARP TO THE PHILIPPIANS (trans. by Glimm)
 MARTYRDOM OF ST. POLYCARP (trans. by Glimm)
 DIDACHE (trans. by Glimm)
 LETTER OF BARNABAS (trans. by Glimm)
 SHEPHERD OF HERMAS (1st printing only; trans. by Marique)
 LETTER TO DIOGNETUS (trans. by Walsh)
 FRAGMENTS OF PAPIAS (1st printing only; trans. by Marique)

VOL. 2: ST. AUGUSTINE (1947)
 CHRISTIAN INSTRUCTION (trans. by Gavigan)
 ADMONITION AND GRACE (trans. by Murray)
 THE CHRISTIAN COMBAT (trans. by Russell)
 FAITH, HOPE, AND CHARITY (trans. by Peebles)

VOL. 3: SALVIAN, THE PRESBYTER (1947)
 GOVERNANCE OF GOD (trans. by O'Sullivan)
 LETTERS (trans. by O'Sullivan)
 FOUR BOOKS OF TIMOTHY TO THE CHURCH (trans. by O'Sullivan)

VOL. 4: ST. AUGUSTINE (1947)
 IMMORTALITY OF THE SOUL (trans. by Schopp)
 MAGNITUDE OF THE SOUL (trans. by McMahon)
 ON MUSIC (trans. by Taliaferro)

ADVANTAGE OF BELIEVING (trans. by Sr. Luanne Meagher)
ON FAITH IN THINGS UNSEEN (trans. by Deferrari and Sr. Mary Francis McDonald)

VOL. 5: ST. AUGUSTINE (1948)
THE HAPPY LIFE (trans. by Schopp)
ANSWER TO SKEPTICS (trans. by Kavanagh)
DIVINE PROVIDENCE AND THE PROBLEM OF EVIL (trans. by Russell)
SOLILOQUES (trans. by Gilligan)

VOL. 6: ST. JUSTIN MARTYR (1948)
FIRST AND SECOND APOLOGY (trans. by Falls)
DIALOGUE WITH TRYPHO (trans. by Falls)
EXHORTATION AND DISCOURSE TO THE GREEKS (trans. by Falls)
THE MONARCHY (trans. by Falls)

VOL. 7: NICETA OF REMESIANA (1949)
WRITINGS (trans. by Walsh and Monohan)
SULPICIUS SEVERUS
WRITINGS (trans. by Peebles)
VINCENT OF LERINS
COMMONITORIES (trans. by Morris)
PROSPER OF AQUITANE
GRACE AND FREE WILL (trans. by O'Donnell)

VOL. 8: ST. AUGUSTINE (1950)
CITY OF GOD, Bks. I-VII (trans. by Walsh, Zema; introduction by Gilson)

VOL. 9: ST. BASIL (1950)
ASCETICAL WORKS (trans. by Sr. M. Monica Wagner)

VOL. 10: TERTULLIAN (1950)
APOLOGETICAL WORKS (vol. I), (trans. by Arbesmann, Sr. Emily Joseph Daly, Quain)
MINUCIUS FELIX
OCTAVIUS (trans. by Arbesmann)

VOL. 11: ST. AUGUSTINE (1951)
COMMENTARY ON THE LORD'S SERMON ON THE MOUNT WITH SEVENTEEN RELATED SERMONS (trans. by Kavanagh)

VOL. 12: ST. AUGUSTINE (1951)
LETTERS 1-82 (vol. 1), (trans. by Sr. Wilfrid Parsons)
VOL. 13: ST. BASIL (1951)
LETTERS 1-185 (vol. 1), (trans. by Deferrari and Sr. Agnes Clare Way)
VOL. 14: ST. AUGUSTINE (1952)
CITY OF GOD, Bks. VIII-XVI (trans. by Walsh and Mtr. Grace Monahan)
VOL. 15: EARLY CHRISTIAN BIOGRAPHIES (1952)
LIFE OF ST. CYPRIAN BY PONTIUS (trans. by Deferrari and Sr. Mary Magdeleine Mueller)
LIFE OF ST AMBROSE, BISHOP OF MILAN, BY PAULINUS (trans. by Lacy)
LIFE OF ST. AUGUSTINE BY POSSIDIUS (trans. by Deferrari and Sr. Mary Magdeleine Mueller)
LIFE OF ST. ANTHONY BY ST. ATHANASIUS (trans. by Sr. Mary Emily Keenan)
LIFE OF ST. PAUL, THE FIRST HERMIT; LIFE OF ST. HILARION; LIFE OF MALCHUS, THE CAPTIVE MONK (trans. by Sr. Marie Liguori Ewald)
LIFE OF EPIPHANIUS BY ENNODIUS (trans. by Sr. Genevieve Marie Cook)
A SERMON ON THE LIFE OF ST. HONORATUS BY ST. HILARY (trans. by Deferrari)
VOL. 16: ST. AUGUSTINE (1952) —Treatises on Various Subjects:
THE CHRISTIAN LIFE, LYING, THE WORK OF MONKS, THE USEFULNESS OF FASTING (trans. by Sr. M. Sarah Muldowney)
AGAINST LYING (trans. by Jaffee)
CONTINENCE (trans. by Sr. Mary Francis McDonald)
PATIENCE (trans. by Sr. Luanne Meagher)
THE EXCELLENCE OF WIDOWHOOD (trans. by Sr. M. Clement Eagan)
THE EIGHT QUESTIONS OF DULCITIUS (trans. by Mary DeFerrari)
VOL. 17: ST. PETER CHRYSOLOGUS (1953)
SELECTED SERMONS (trans. by Ganss)
ST. VALERIAN
HOMILIES (trans. by Ganss)

VOL. 18: ST. AUGUSTINE (1953)
LETTERS 83-130 (vol. 2), (trans. by Sr. Wilfrid Parsons)

VOL. 19: EUSEBIUS PAMPHILI (1953)
ECCLESIASTICAL HISTORY, Bks. 1-5 (trans. by Deferrari)

VOL. 20: ST. AUGUSTINE (1953)
LETTERS 131-164 (vol. 3), (trans. by Sr. Wilfrid Parsons)

VOL. 21: ST. AUGUSTINE (1953)
CONFESSIONS (trans. by Bourke)

VOL. 22: ST. GREGORY OF NAZIANZEN and ST. AMBROSE (1953)
FUNERAL ORATIONS (trans. by McCauley, Sullivan, McGuire, Deferrari)

VOL. 23: CLEMENT OF ALEXANDRIA (1954)
CHRIST, THE EDUCATOR (trans. by Wood)

VOL. 24: ST. AUGUSTINE (1954)
CITY OF GOD, Bks. XVII-XXII (trans. by Walsh and Honan)

VOL. 25: ST. HILARY OF POITIERS (1954)
THE TRINITY (trans. by McKenna)

VOL. 26: ST. AMBROSE (1954)
LETTERS 1-91 (trans. by Sr. M. Melchior Beyenka)

VOL. 27: ST. AUGUSTINE (1955) —Treatises on Marriage and Other Subjects:
THE GOOD OF MARRIAGE (trans. by Wilcox)
ADULTEROUS MARRIAGES (trans. by Huegelmeyer)
HOLY VIRGINITY (trans. by McQuade)
FAITH AND WORKS, THE CREED, IN ANSWER TO THE JEWS (trans. by Sr. Marie Liguori Ewald)
FAITH AND THE CREED (trans. by Russell)
THE CARE TO BE TAKEN FOR THE DEAD (trans. by Lacy)
THE DIVINATION OF DEMONS (trans. by Brown)

VOL. 28: ST. BASIL (1955)
LETTERS 186-368 (vol. 2), (trans. by Sr. Agnes Clare Way)

VOL. 29: EUSEBIUS PAMPHILI (1955)
ECCLESIASTICAL HISTORY, Bks. 6-10 (trans. by Deferrari)

VOL. 30: ST. AUGUSTINE (1955)
LETTERS 165-203 (vol. 4), (trans. by Sr. Wilfrid Parsons)

VOL. 31: ST. CAESARIUS OF ARLES (1956)
SERMONS 1-80 (vol. 1), (trans. by Sr. Mary Magdeleine Mueller)

VOL. 32: ST. AUGUSTINE (1956)
LETTERS 204-270 (vol. 5), (trans. by Sr. Wilfrid Parsons)

VOL. 33: ST. JOHN CHRYSOSTOM (1957)
HOMILIES 1-47 (vol. 1), (trans. by Sr. Thomas Aquinas Goggin)

VOL. 34: ST. LEO THE GREAT (1957)
LETTERS (trans. by Hunt)

VOL. 35: ST. AUGUSTINE (1957)
AGAINST JULIAN (trans. by Schumacher)

VOL. 36: ST. CYPRIAN (1958)
TREATISES (trans. by Deferrari, Sr. Angela Elizabeth Keenan, Mahoney, Sr. George Edward Conway)

VOL. 37: ST. JOHN OF DAMASCUS (1958)
FOUNT OF KNOWLEDGE, ON HERESIES, THE ORTHODOX FAITH (trans. by Chase)

VOL. 38: ST. AUGUSTINE (1959)
SERMONS ON THE LITURGICAL SEASONS (trans. by Sr. M. Sarah Muldowney)

VOL. 39: ST. GREGORY THE GREAT (1959)
DIALOGUES (trans. by Zimmerman)

VOL. 40: TERTULLIAN (1959)
DISCIPLINARY, MORAL, AND ASCETICAL WORKS (trans. by Arbesmann, Quain, Sr. Emily Joseph Daly)

VOL. 41: ST. JOHN CHRYSOSTOM (1960)
HOMILIES 48-88 (vol. 2), (trans. by Sr. Thomas Aquinas Goggin)

VOL. 42: ST. AMBROSE (1961)
HEXAMERON, PARADISE, AND CAIN AND ABEL (trans. by Savage)

VOL. 43: PRUDENTIUS (1962)
POEMS (vol. 1), (trans. by Sr. M. Clement Eagan)

VOL. 44: ST. AMBROSE (1963)
THEOLOGICAL AND DOGMATIC WORKS (trans. by Deferrari)

VOL. 45: ST. AUGUSTINE (1963)
THE TRINITY (trans. by McKenna)

VOL. 46: ST. BASIL (1963)
EXEGETIC HOMILIES (trans. by Sr. Agnes Clare Way)

VOL. 47: ST. CAESARIUS OF ARLES (1964)
SERMONS 81-186 (vol. 2), (trans. by Sr. Mary Magdeleine Mueller)

VOL. 48: ST. JEROME (1964)
HOMILIES 1-59 (vol. 1), (trans. by Sr. Marie Liguori Ewald)

VOL. 49: LACTANTIUS (1964)
THE DIVINE INSTITUTES, Bks. I-VII (trans. by Sr. Mary Francis McDonald)

VOL. 50: OROSIUS (1964)
SEVEN BOOKS AGAINST THE PAGANS (trans. by Deferrari)

VOL. 51: ST. CYPRIAN (1965)
LETTERS (trans. by Sr. Rose Bernard Donna)

VOL. 52: PRUDENTIUS (1965)
POEMS (vol. 2), (trans. by Sr. M. Clement Eagan)

VOL. 53: ST. JEROME (1965)
DOGMATIC AND POLEMICAL WORKS (trans. by John N. Hritzu)

VOL. 54: LACTANTIUS (1965)
THE MINOR WORKS (trans. by Sr. Mary Francis McDonald)

VOL. 55: EUGIPPIUS (1965)
LIFE OF ST. SEVERIN (trans. by Bieler)

www.ingramcontent.com/pod-product-compliance
Lightning Source LLC
Chambersburg PA
CBHW020324010526
44107CB00054B/1968